NICKELODEON

Spon
squarepants™

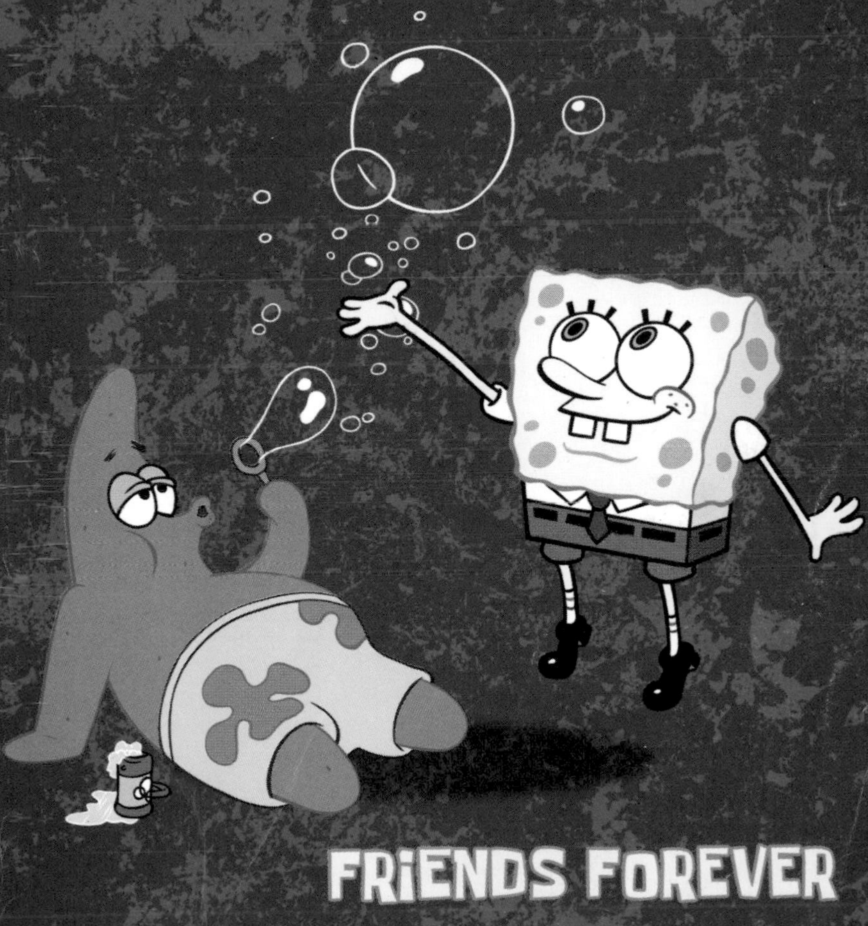

FRIENDS FOREVER

Contributing Editors - Kimberlee Smith & Paul Morrissey
Graphic Design and Lettering - Dave Snow
Cover Layout - Raymond Makowski
Graphic Artists - Anna Kernbaum & Tomás Montalvo-Lagos

Editor - Elizabeth Hurchalla
Managing Editor - Jill Freshney
Production Coordinator - Antonio DePietro
Production Manager - Jennifer Miller
Art Director - Matt Alford
Editorial Director - Jeremy Ross
VP of Production - Ron Klamert
President & C.O.O. - John Parker
Publisher & C.E.O. - Stuart Levy

Email: editor@TOKYOPOP.com
Come visit us online at www.TOKYOPOP.com

A ⊙**TOKYOPOP** Cine-Manga™
TOKYOPOP Inc.
5900 Wilshire Blvd., Suite 2000, Los Angeles, CA 90036

ISBN: 1-59182-399-4

First TOKYOPOP® printing: November 2003

10 9 8 7 6 5 4 3 2 1

Printed in Canada

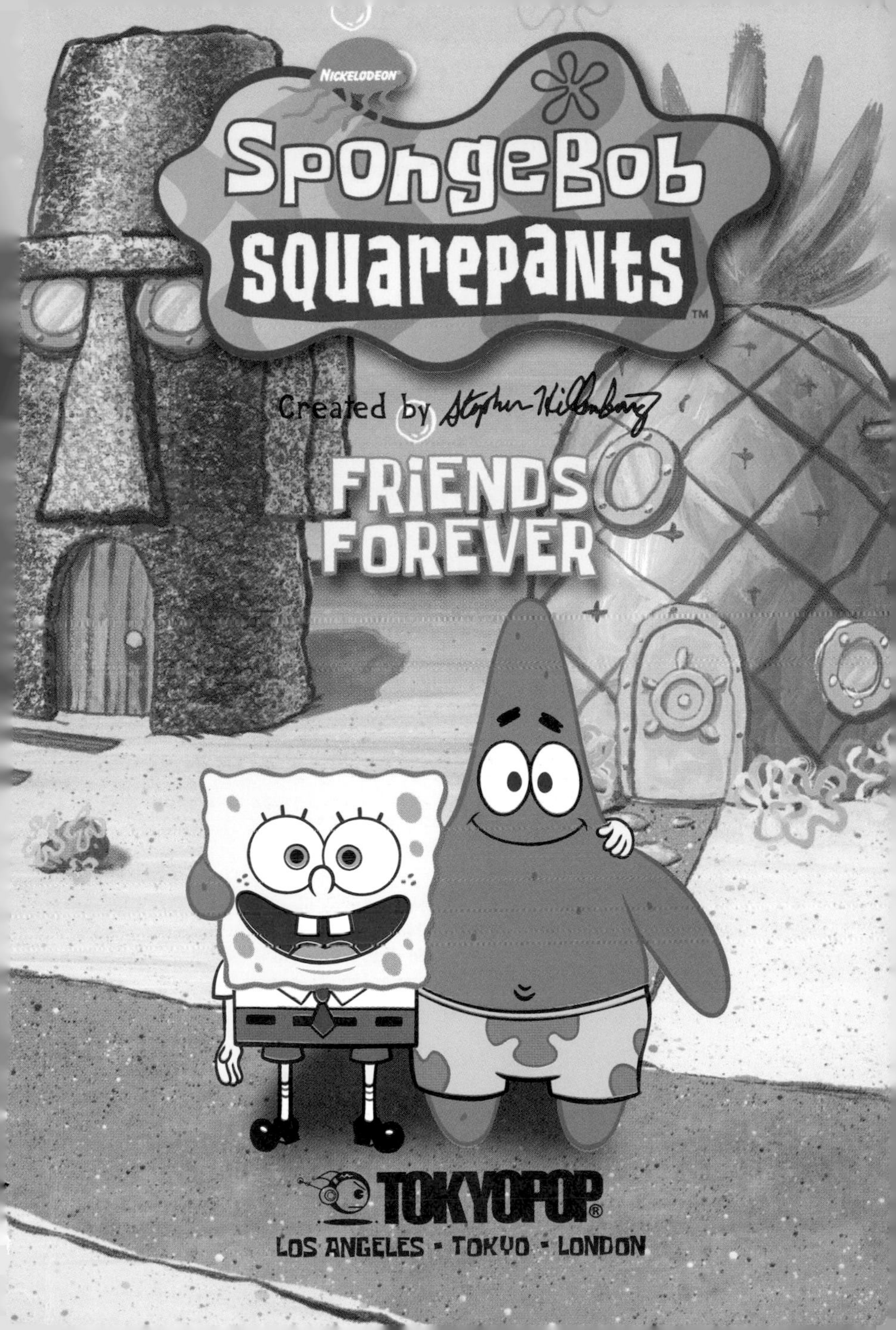
NICKELODEON
SpongeBob SquarePants™
Created by Stephen Hillenburg
FRIENDS FOREVER
TOKYOPOP®
LOS ANGELES • TOKYO • LONDON

SpongeBob™ SquarePants

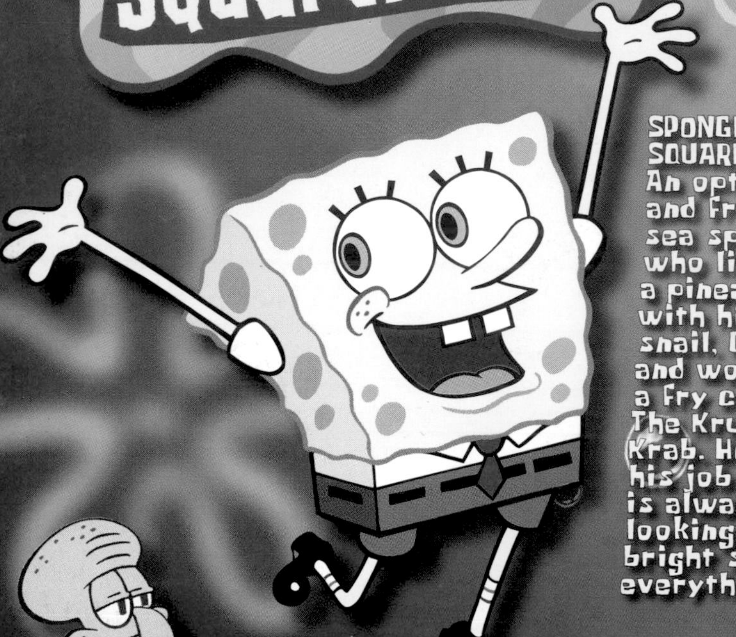

SPONGEBOB SQUAREPANTS: An optimistic and friendly sea sponge who lives in a pineapple with his snail, Gary, and works as a fry cook at The Krusty Krab. He loves his job and is always looking on the bright side of everything.

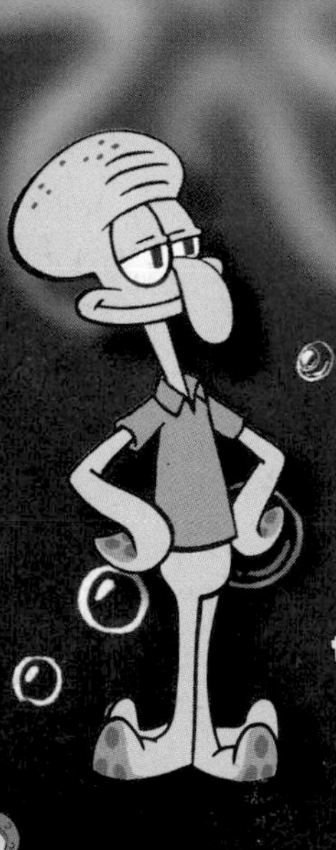

SQUIDWARD TENTACLES: A squid who works as the cashier at The Krusty Krab. Unlike SpongeBob, Squidward tends to be negative about everything.

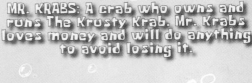

MR. KRABS: A crab who owns and runs The Krusty Krab. Mr. Krabs loves money and will do anything to avoid losing it.

GARY: SpongeBob's pet snail. Meows like a cat.

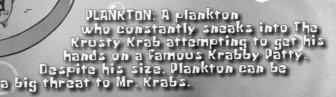

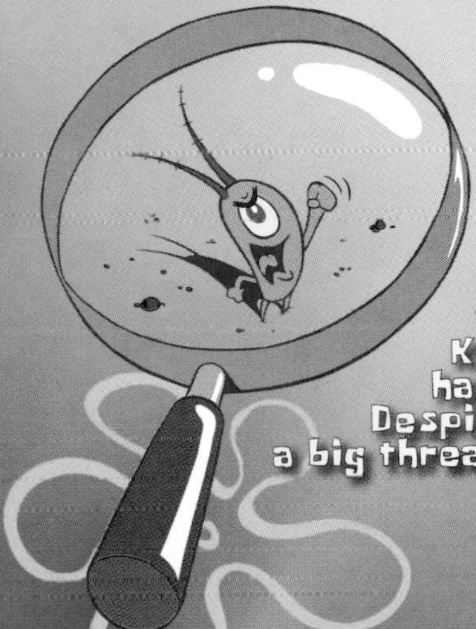

PLANKTON: A plankton who constantly sneaks into The Krusty Krab attempting to get his hands on a famous Krabby Patty. Despite his size, Plankton can be a big threat to Mr. Krabs.

PATRICK STAR: A starfish who is SpongeBob's best friend and neighbor.

SpongeBob SquarePants

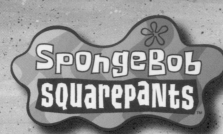

FRIENDS FOREVER

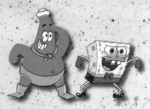

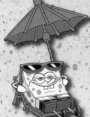

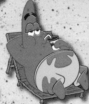

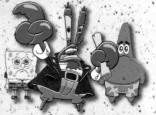

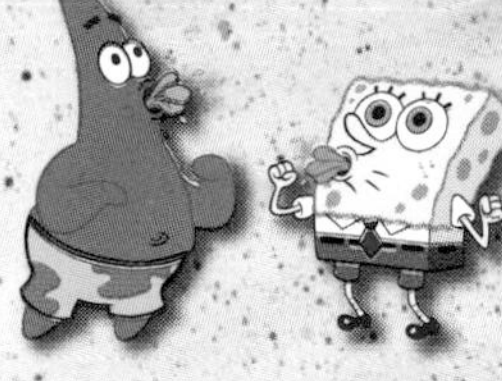

SpongeBob SquarePants

Spongeguard On Duty

by Jay Lender, Sam Henderson
and Mark O'Hare

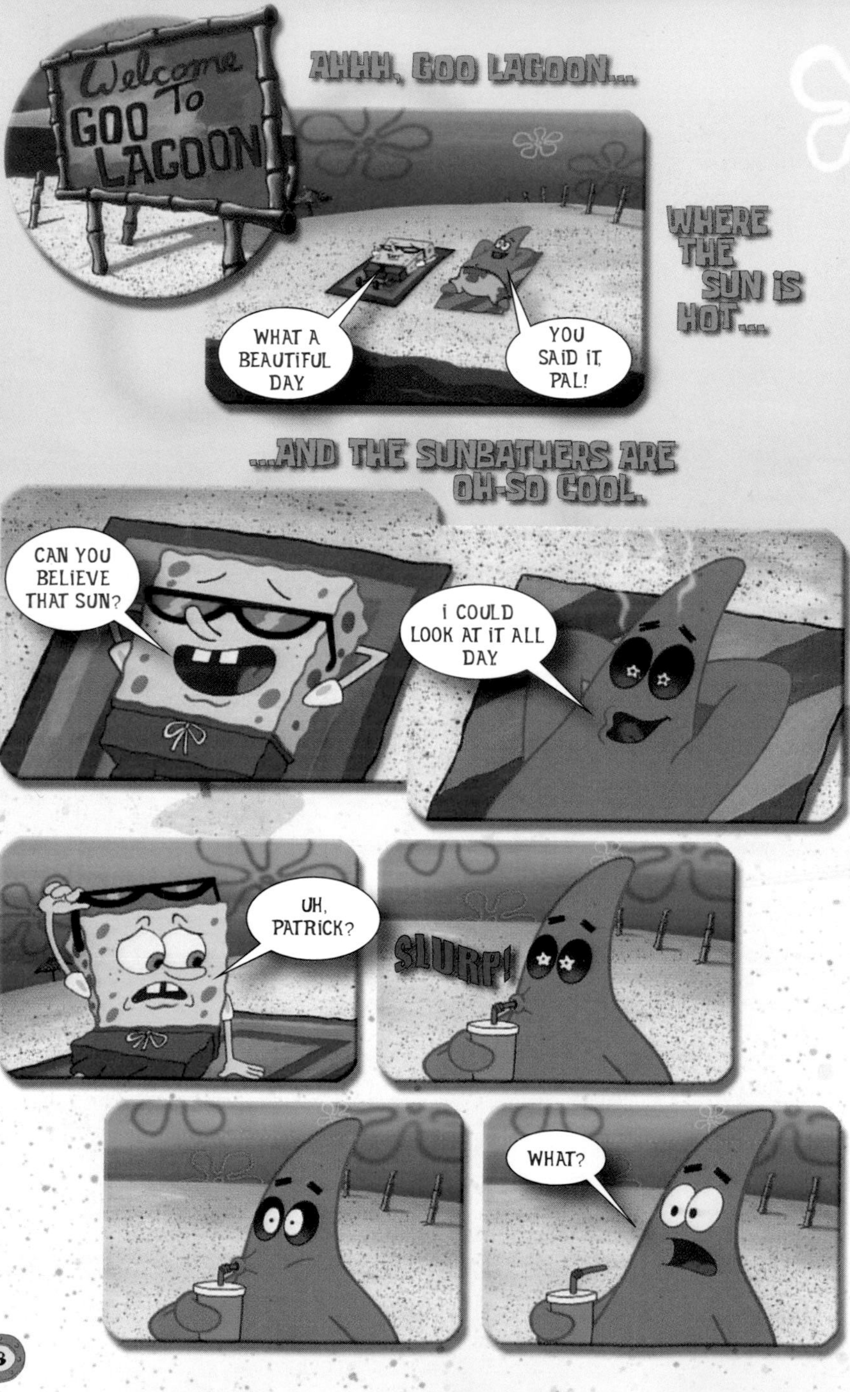
Welcome To GOO LAGOON
AHHH, GOO LAGOON...
WHAT A BEAUTIFUL DAY.
YOU SAID IT, PAL!
WHERE THE SUN IS HOT...
...AND THE SUNBATHERS ARE OH-SO COOL.
CAN YOU BELIEVE THAT SUN?
I COULD LOOK AT IT ALL DAY.
UH, PATRICK?
SLURP!
WHAT?

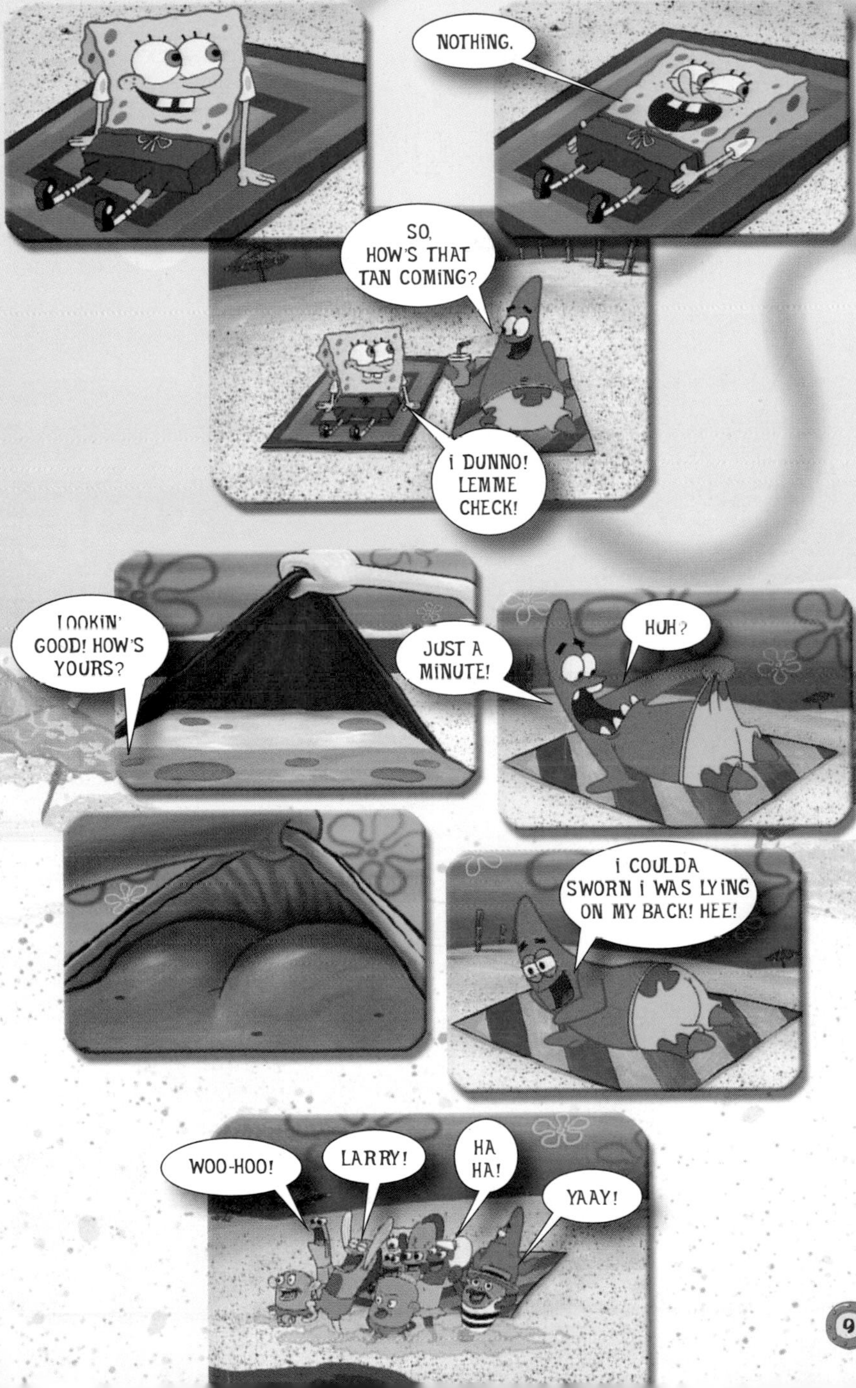
NOTHING.
SO, HOW'S THAT TAN COMING?
I DUNNO! LEMME CHECK!
LOOKIN' GOOD! HOW'S YOURS?
JUST A MINUTE!
HUH?
I COULDA SWORN I WAS LYING ON MY BACK! HEE!
WOO-HOO!
LARRY!
HA HA!
YAAY!

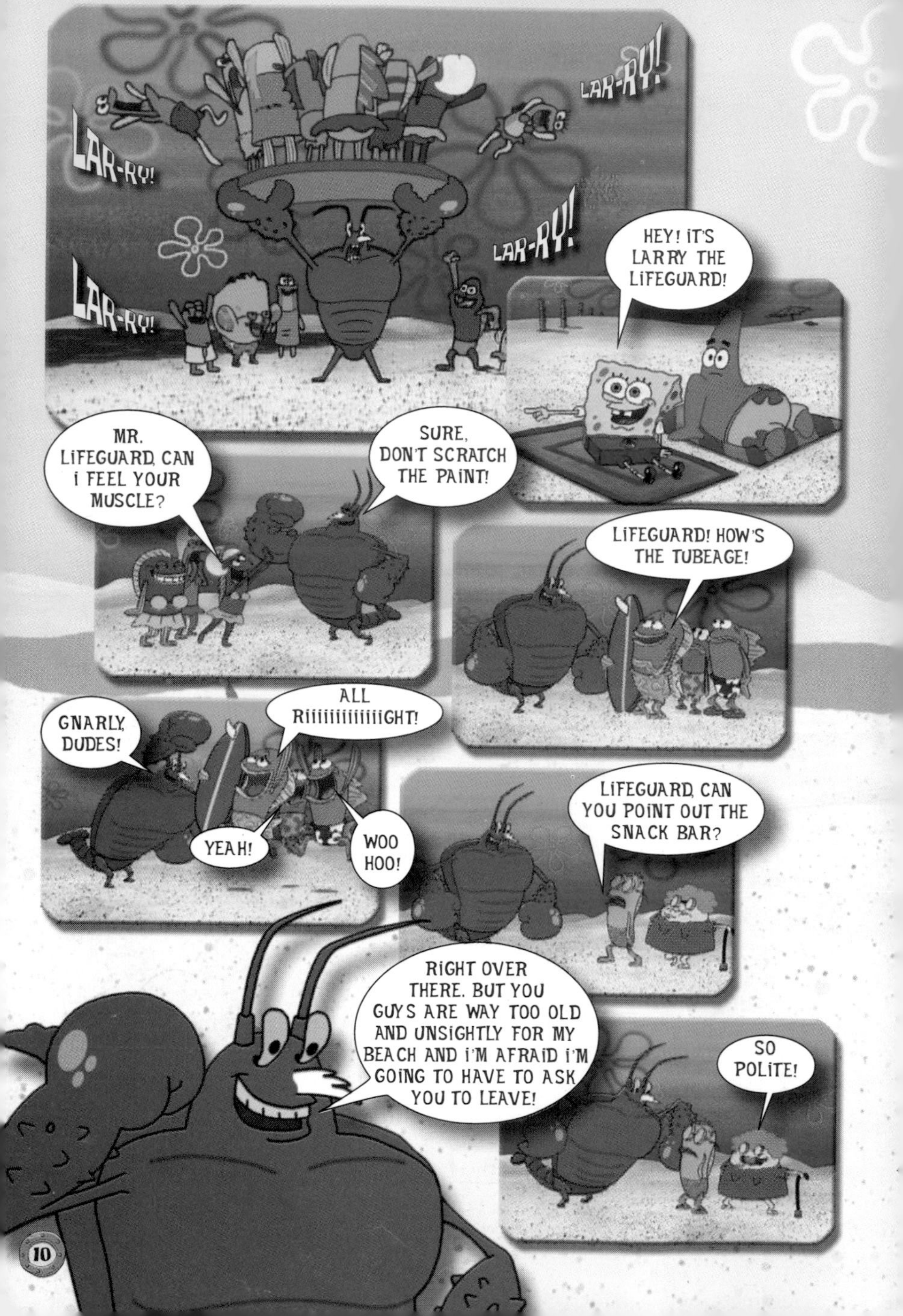
LAR-RY!
LAR-RY!
LAR-RY!
LAR-RY!
HEY! IT'S LARRY THE LIFEGUARD!
MR. LIFEGUARD, CAN I FEEL YOUR MUSCLE?
SURE, DON'T SCRATCH THE PAINT!
LIFEGUARD! HOW'S THE TUBEAGE!
GNARLY, DUDES!
ALL Riiiiiiiiiiiiiight!
YEAH!
WOO HOO!
LIFEGUARD, CAN YOU POINT OUT THE SNACK BAR?
RIGHT OVER THERE. BUT YOU GUYS ARE WAY TOO OLD AND UNSIGHTLY FOR MY BEACH AND I'M AFRAID I'M GOING TO HAVE TO ASK YOU TO LEAVE!
SO POLITE!

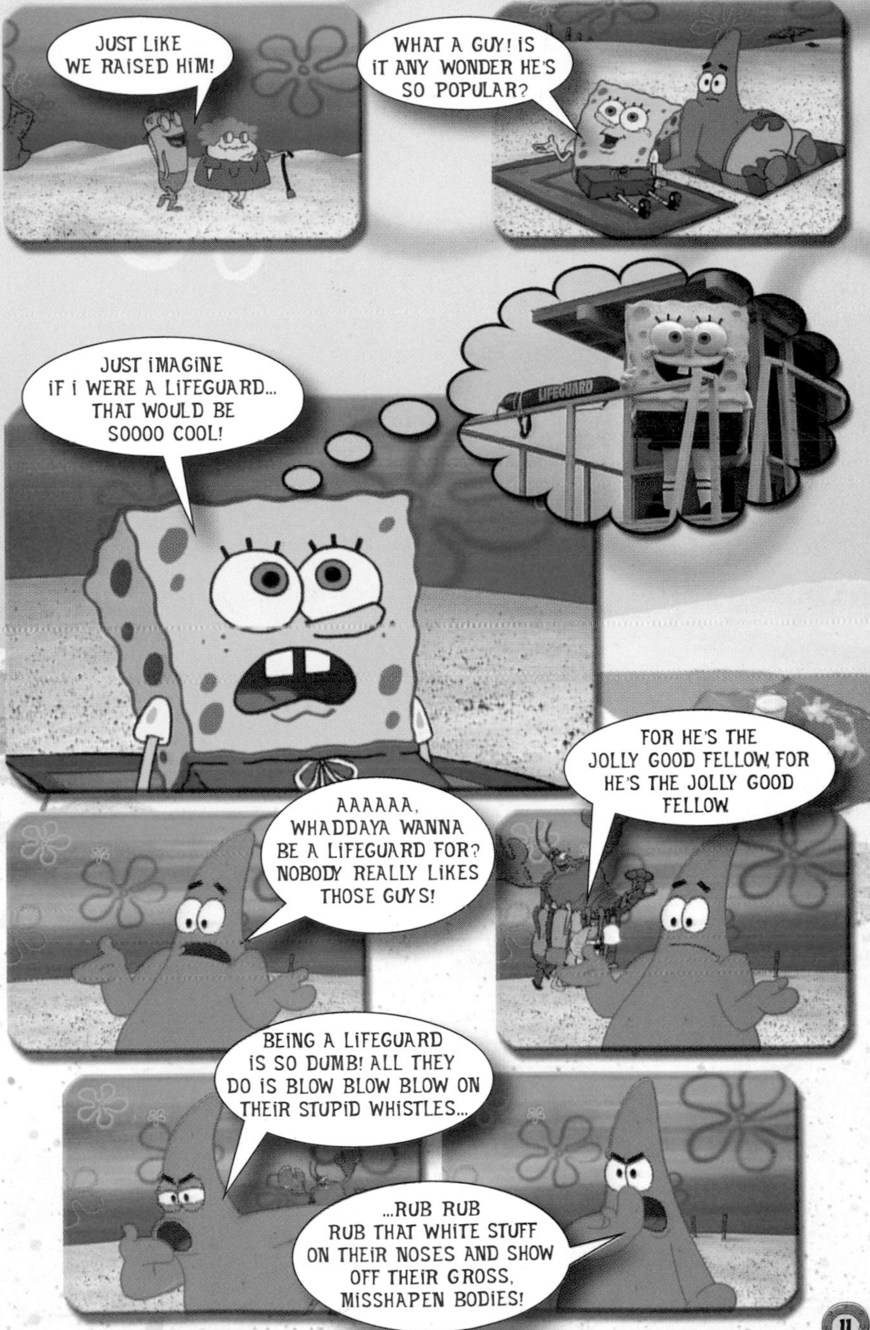
JUST LIKE WE RAISED HIM!
WHAT A GUY! IS IT ANY WONDER HE'S SO POPULAR?
JUST IMAGINE IF I WERE A LIFEGUARD... THAT WOULD BE SOOOO COOL!
LIFEGUARD
AAAAAA, WHADDAYA WANNA BE A LIFEGUARD FOR? NOBODY REALLY LIKES THOSE GUYS!
FOR HE'S THE JOLLY GOOD FELLOW, FOR HE'S THE JOLLY GOOD FELLOW.
BEING A LIFEGUARD IS SO DUMB! ALL THEY DO IS BLOW BLOW BLOW ON THEIR STUPID WHISTLES...
...RUB RUB RUB THAT WHITE STUFF ON THEIR NOSES AND SHOW OFF THEIR GROSS, MISSHAPEN BODIES!

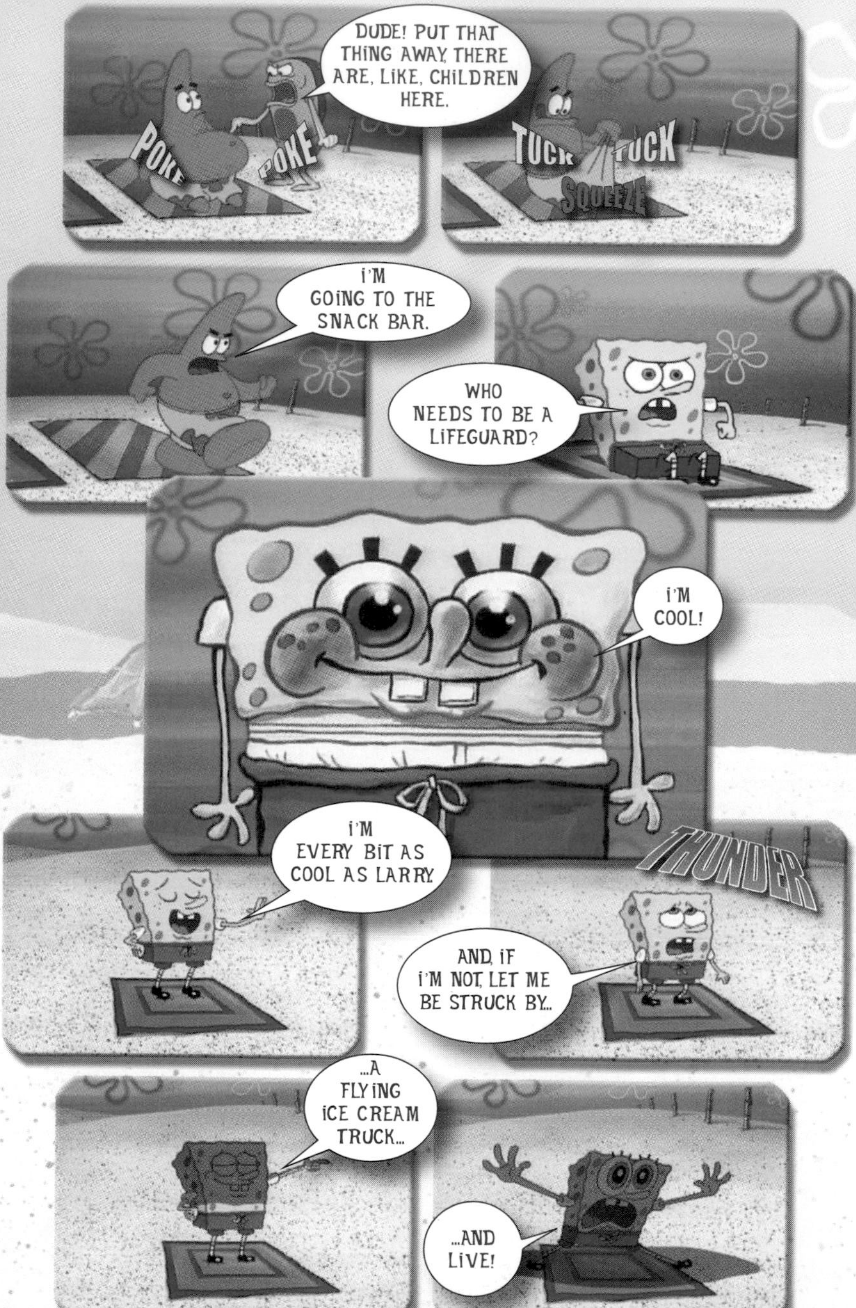
POKE
POKE
DUDE! PUT THAT THING AWAY. THERE ARE, LIKE, CHILDREN HERE.
TUCK
TUCK
SQUEEZE
I'M GOING TO THE SNACK BAR.
WHO NEEDS TO BE A LIFEGUARD?
I'M COOL!
I'M EVERY BIT AS COOL AS LARRY.
THUNDER
AND, IF I'M NOT, LET ME BE STRUCK BY...
...A FLYING ICE CREAM TRUCK...
...AND LIVE!

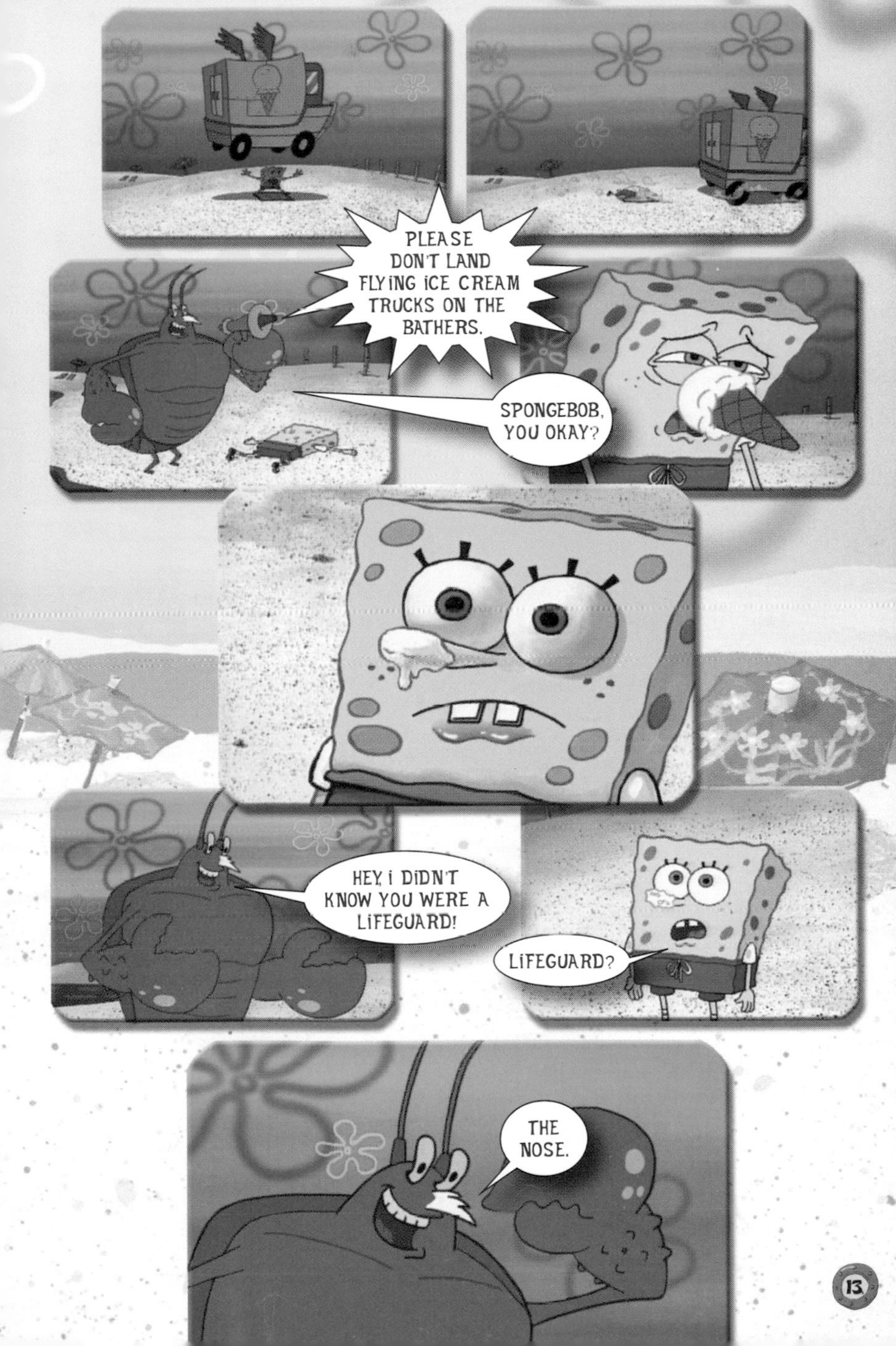
PLEASE DON'T LAND FLYiNG iCE CREAM TRUCKS ON THE BATHERS.
SPONGEBOB, YOU OKAY?
HEY, i DiDN'T KNOW YOU WERE A LiFEGUARD!
LiFEGUARD?
THE NOSE.

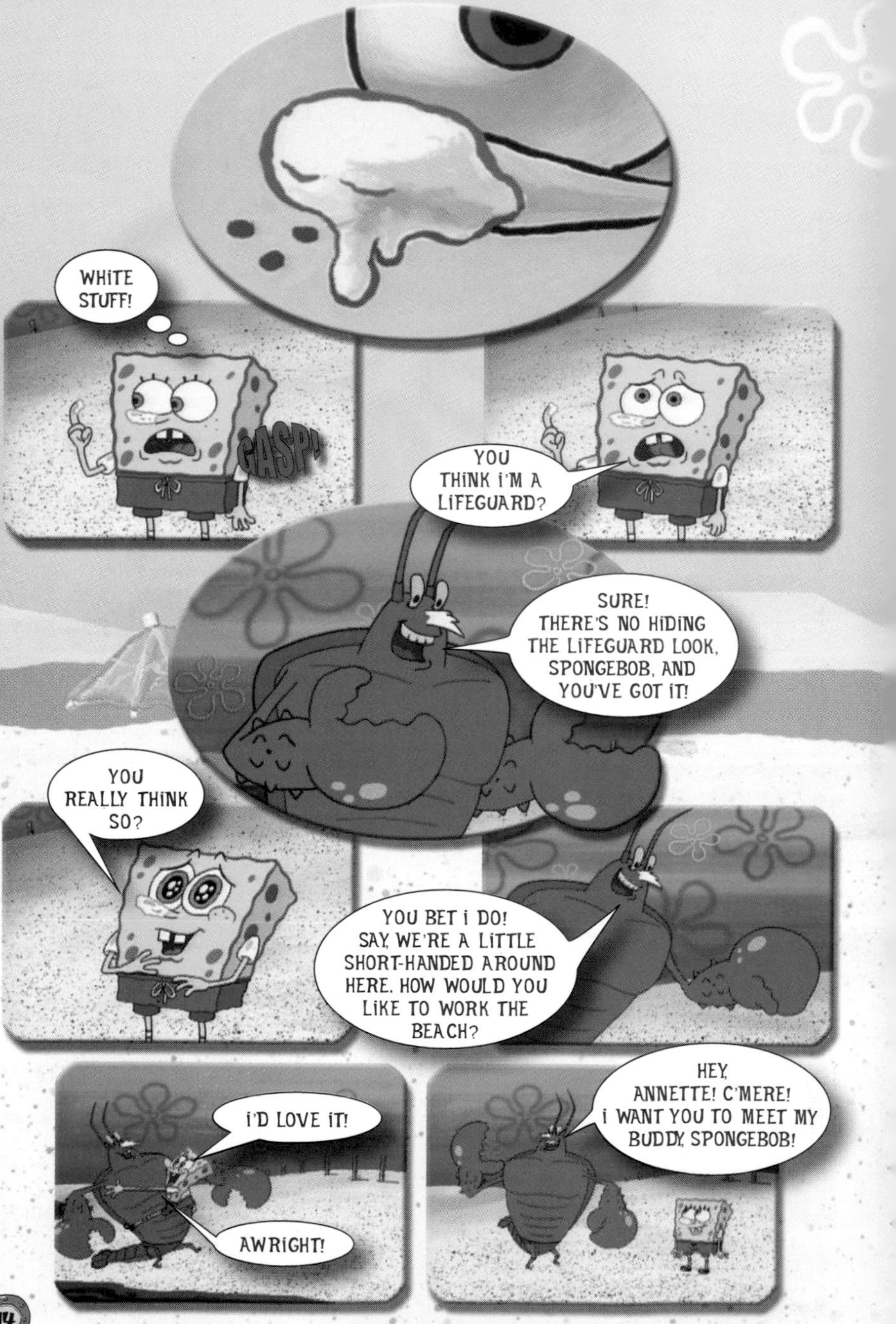
WHITE STUFF!
GASP!
YOU THINK I'M A LIFEGUARD?
SURE! THERE'S NO HIDING THE LIFEGUARD LOOK, SPONGEBOB, AND YOU'VE GOT IT!
YOU REALLY THINK SO?
YOU BET I DO! SAY, WE'RE A LITTLE SHORT-HANDED AROUND HERE. HOW WOULD YOU LIKE TO WORK THE BEACH?
I'D LOVE IT!
AWRIGHT!
HEY, ANNETTE! C'MERE! I WANT YOU TO MEET MY BUDDY, SPONGEBOB!

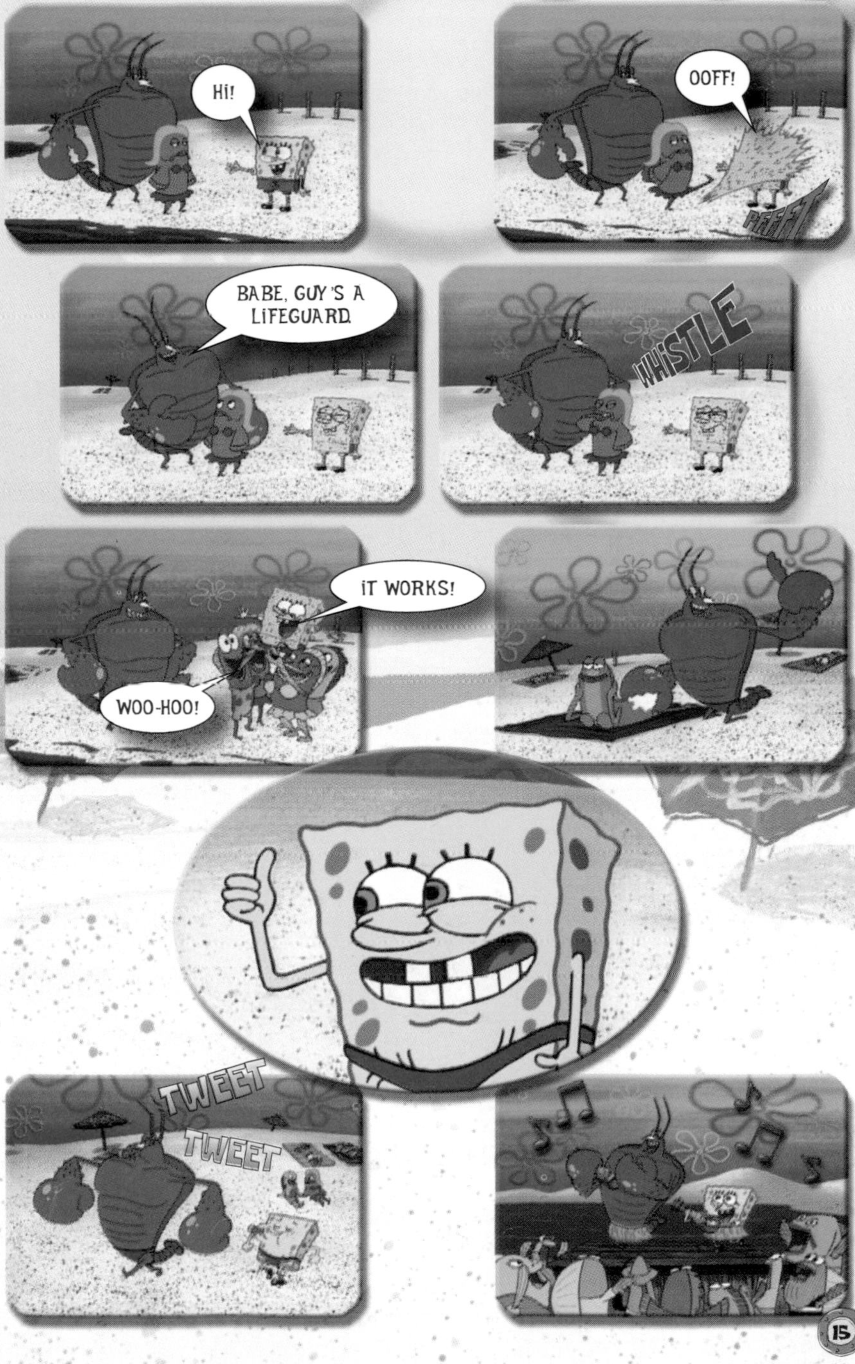

Hi!
OOFF!
PFFFT
BABE, GUY'S A LIFEGUARD.
WHISTLE
IT WORKS!
WOO-HOO!
TWEET
TWEET

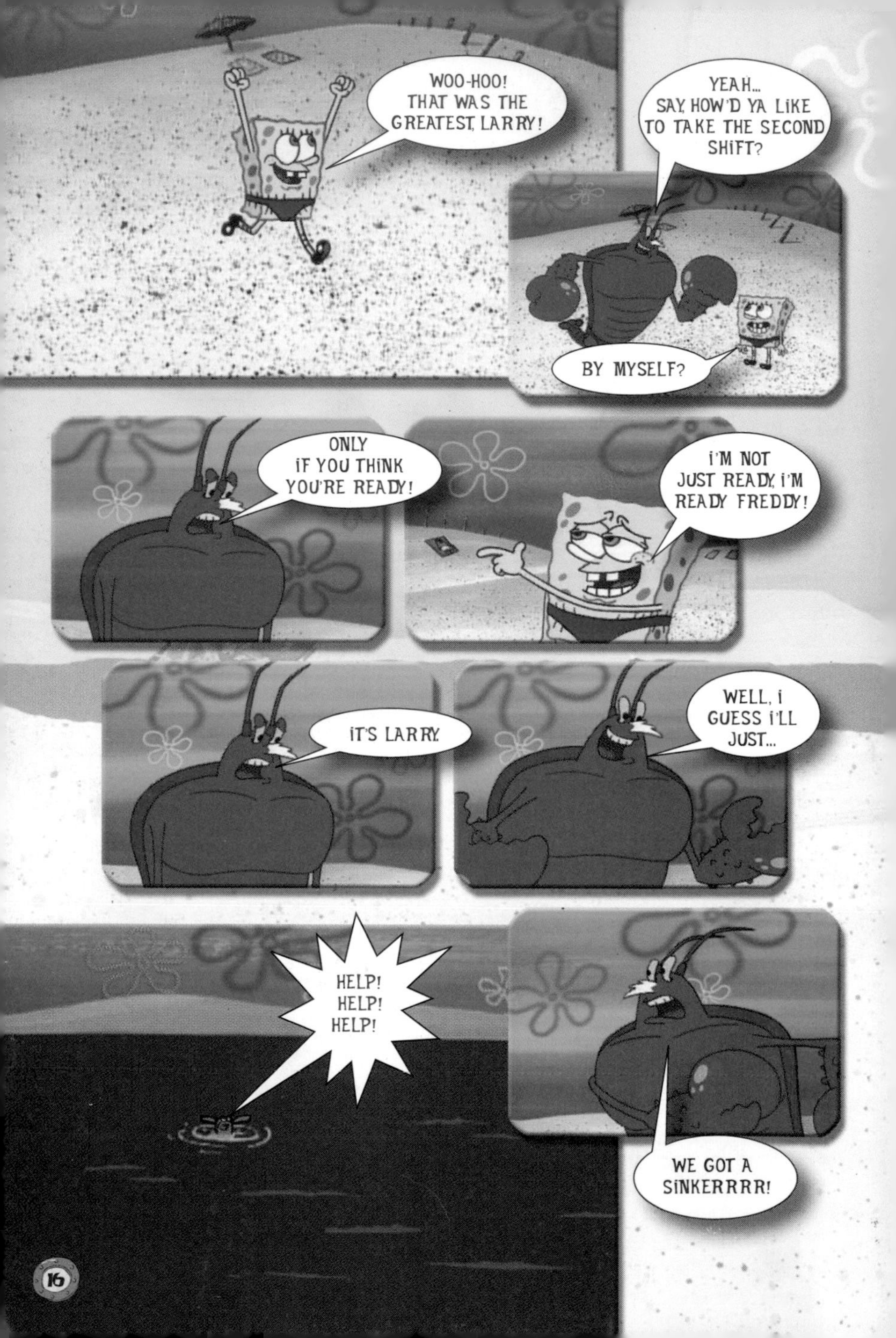
WOO-HOO! THAT WAS THE GREATEST, LARRY!
YEAH... SAY, HOW'D YA LIKE TO TAKE THE SECOND SHIFT?
BY MYSELF?
ONLY IF YOU THINK YOU'RE READY!
I'M NOT JUST READY, I'M READY FREDDY!
IT'S LARRY.
WELL, I GUESS I'LL JUST...
HELP! HELP! HELP!
WE GOT A SINKERRRR!

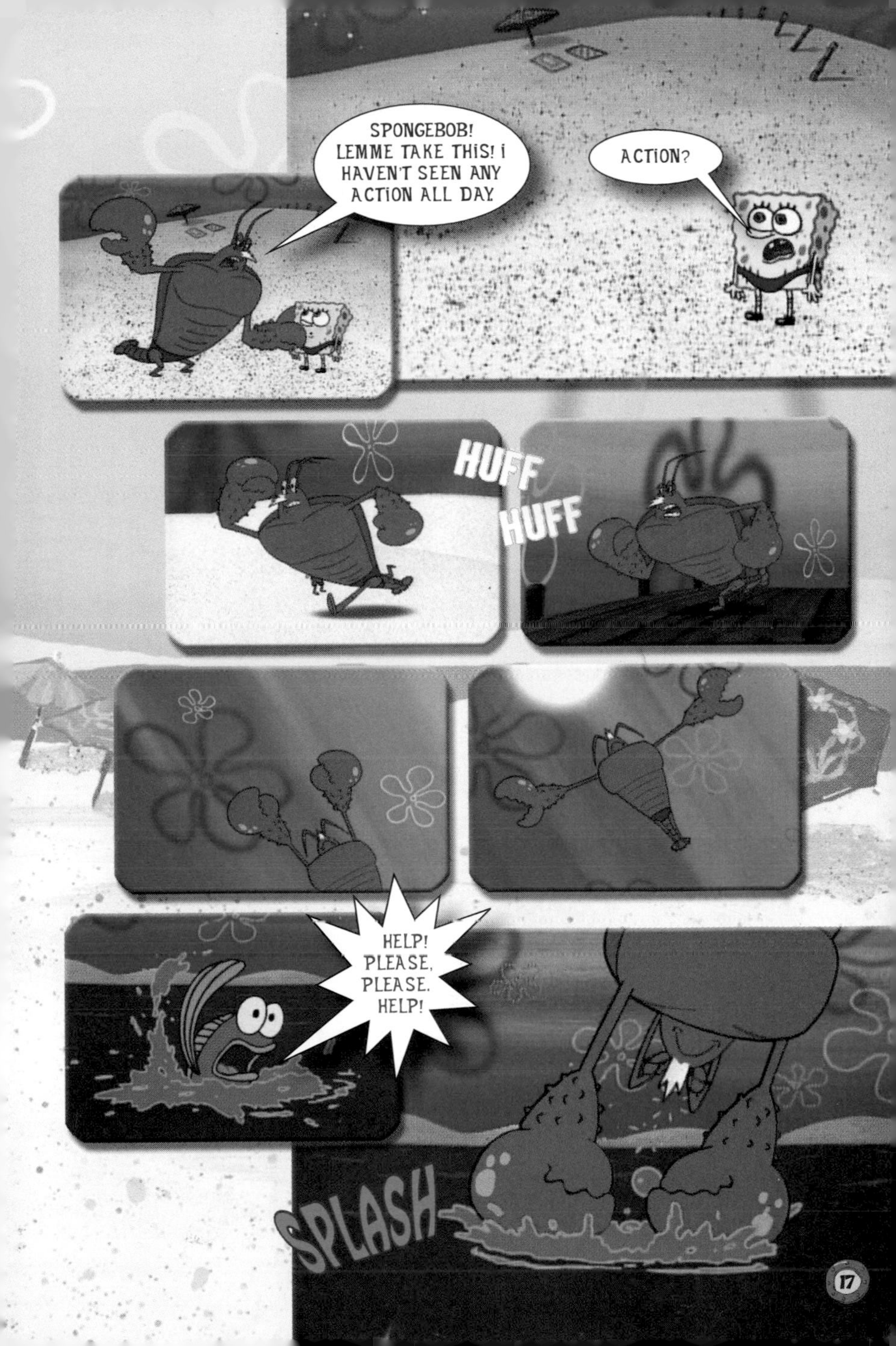

SPONGEBOB! LEMME TAKE THIS! I HAVEN'T SEEN ANY ACTION ALL DAY.
ACTION?
HUFF
HUFF
HELP! PLEASE, PLEASE. HELP!
SPLASH

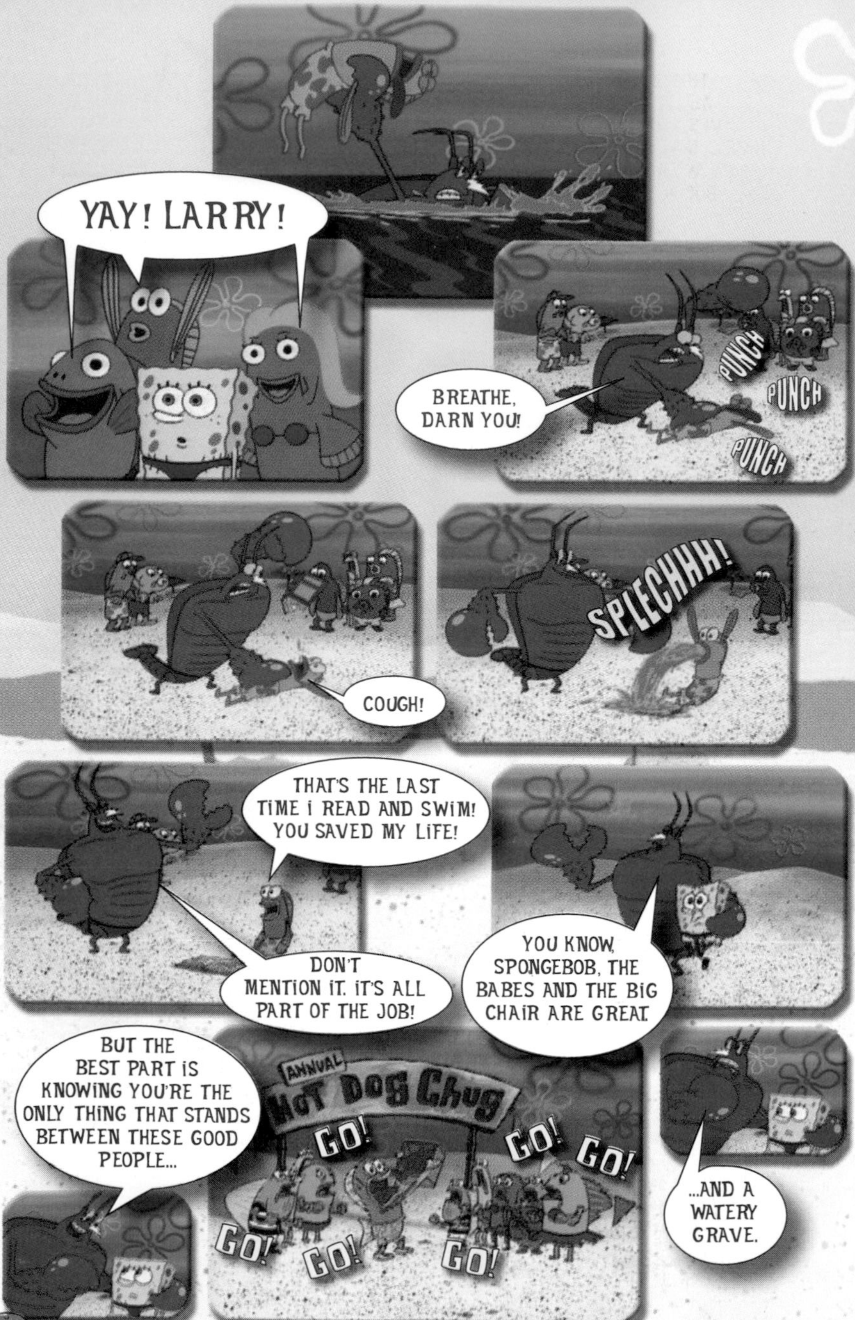
YAY! LARRY!
BREATHE, DARN YOU!
PUNCH
PUNCH
PUNCH
COUGH!
SPLECHHH!
THAT'S THE LAST TIME I READ AND SWIM! YOU SAVED MY LIFE!
DON'T MENTION IT. IT'S ALL PART OF THE JOB!
YOU KNOW, SPONGEBOB, THE BABES AND THE BIG CHAIR ARE GREAT.
BUT THE BEST PART IS KNOWING YOU'RE THE ONLY THING THAT STANDS BETWEEN THESE GOOD PEOPLE...
ANNUAL
HoT Dog Chug
GO!
GO!
GO!
GO!
GO!
GO!
...AND A WATERY GRAVE.

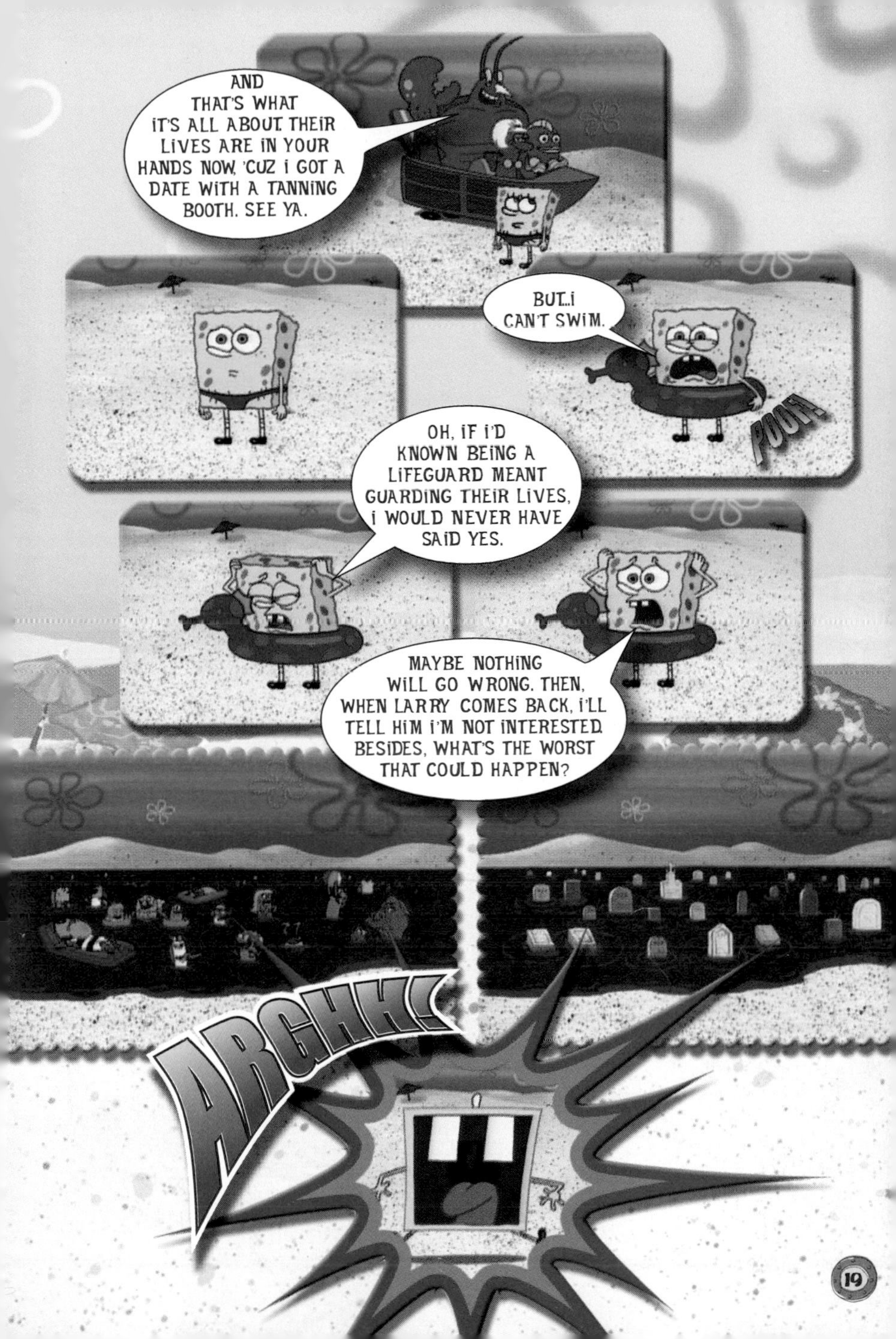
AND THAT'S WHAT IT'S ALL ABOUT. THEIR LIVES ARE IN YOUR HANDS NOW, 'CUZ I GOT A DATE WITH A TANNING BOOTH. SEE YA.
BUT...I CAN'T SWIM.
POOF!
OH, IF I'D KNOWN BEING A LIFEGUARD MEANT GUARDING THEIR LIVES, I WOULD NEVER HAVE SAID YES.
MAYBE NOTHING WILL GO WRONG. THEN, WHEN LARRY COMES BACK, I'LL TELL HIM I'M NOT INTERESTED. BESIDES, WHAT'S THE WORST THAT COULD HAPPEN?
ARGHH!

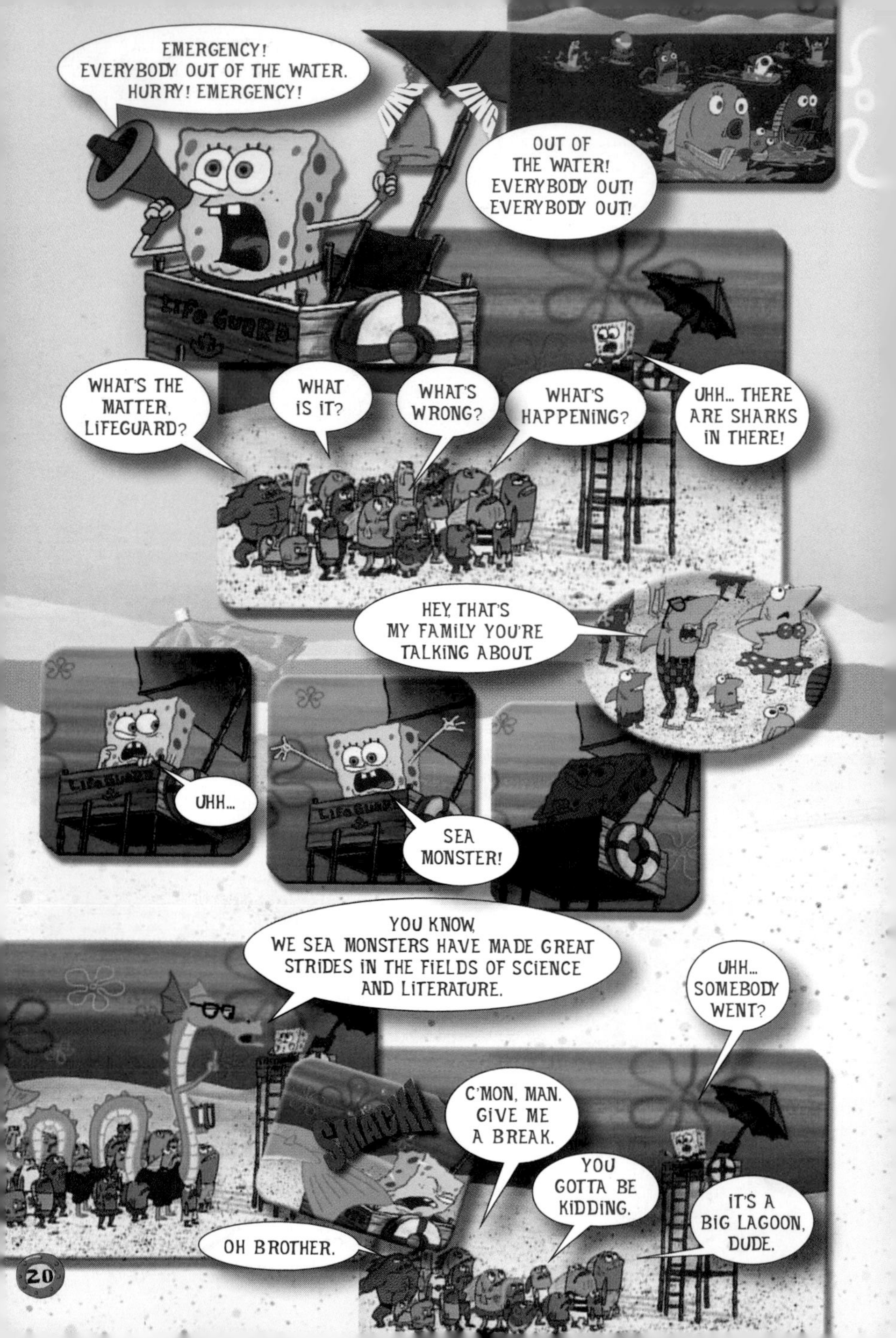
EMERGENCY! EVERYBODY OUT OF THE WATER. HURRY! EMERGENCY!
DING DING
OUT OF THE WATER! EVERYBODY OUT! EVERYBODY OUT!
LIFE GUARD
WHAT'S THE MATTER, LIFEGUARD?
WHAT IS IT?
WHAT'S WRONG?
WHAT'S HAPPENING?
UHH... THERE ARE SHARKS IN THERE!
HEY, THAT'S MY FAMILY YOU'RE TALKING ABOUT.
UHH...
SEA MONSTER!
YOU KNOW, WE SEA MONSTERS HAVE MADE GREAT STRIDES IN THE FIELDS OF SCIENCE AND LITERATURE.
SMACK!
OH BROTHER.
C'MON, MAN. GIVE ME A BREAK.
YOU GOTTA BE KIDDING.
UHH... SOMEBODY WENT?
IT'S A BIG LAGOON, DUDE.

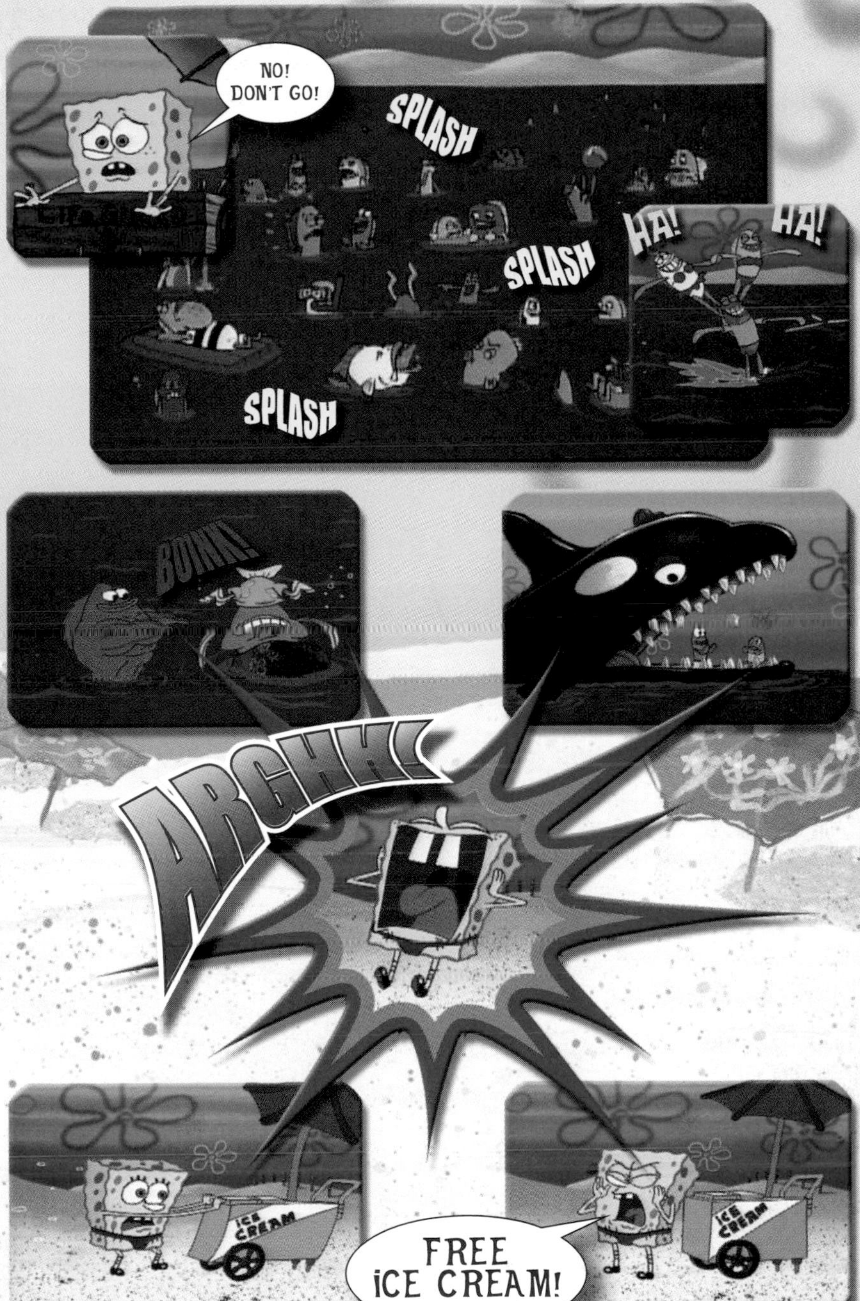
NO! DON'T GO!
SPLASH
SPLASH
SPLASH
HA! HA!
ARGHH!
ICE CREAM
FREE ICE CREAM!
ICE CREAM

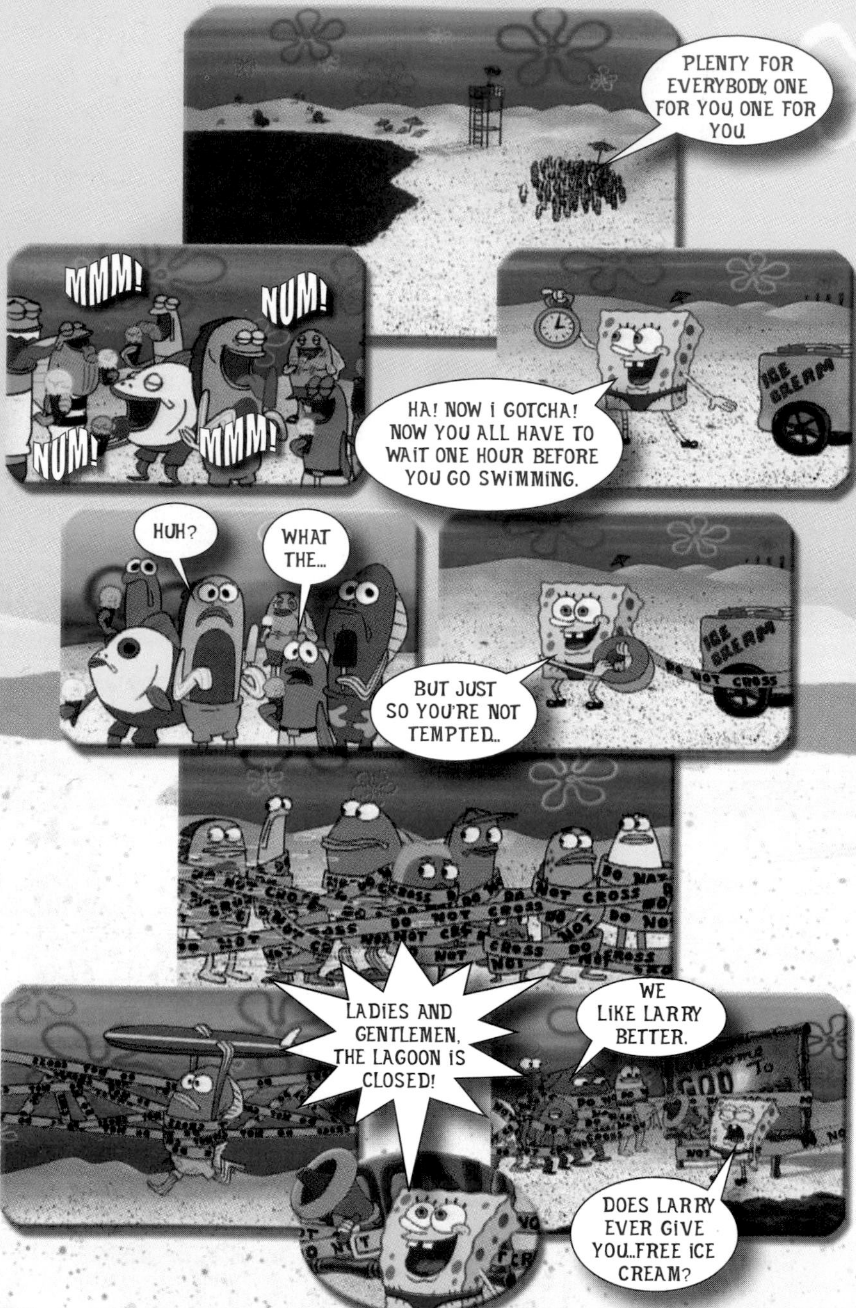
PLENTY FOR EVERYBODY, ONE FOR YOU, ONE FOR YOU.
MMM!
NUM!
NUM!
MMM!
HA! NOW I GOTCHA! NOW YOU ALL HAVE TO WAIT ONE HOUR BEFORE YOU GO SWIMMING.
HUH?
WHAT THE...
BUT JUST SO YOU'RE NOT TEMPTED...
LADIES AND GENTLEMEN, THE LAGOON IS CLOSED!
WE LIKE LARRY BETTER.
DOES LARRY EVER GIVE YOU...FREE ICE CREAM?

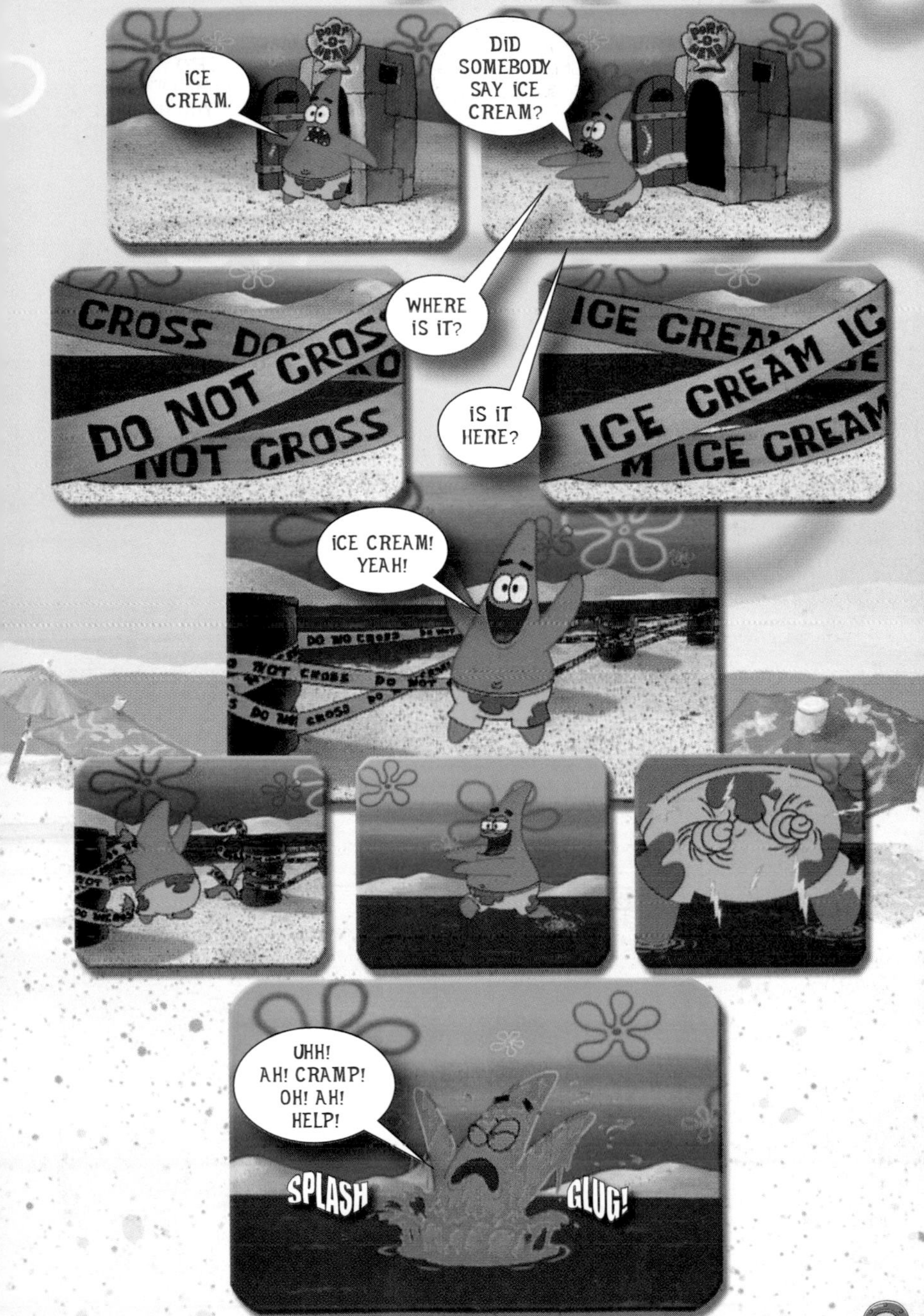
ICE CREAM.
DID SOMEBODY SAY ICE CREAM?
DO NOT CROSS
NOT CROSS
WHERE IS IT?
IS IT HERE?
ICE CREAM
ICE CREAM
ICE CREAM! YEAH!
UHH! AH! CRAMP! OH! AH! HELP!
SPLASH
GLUG!

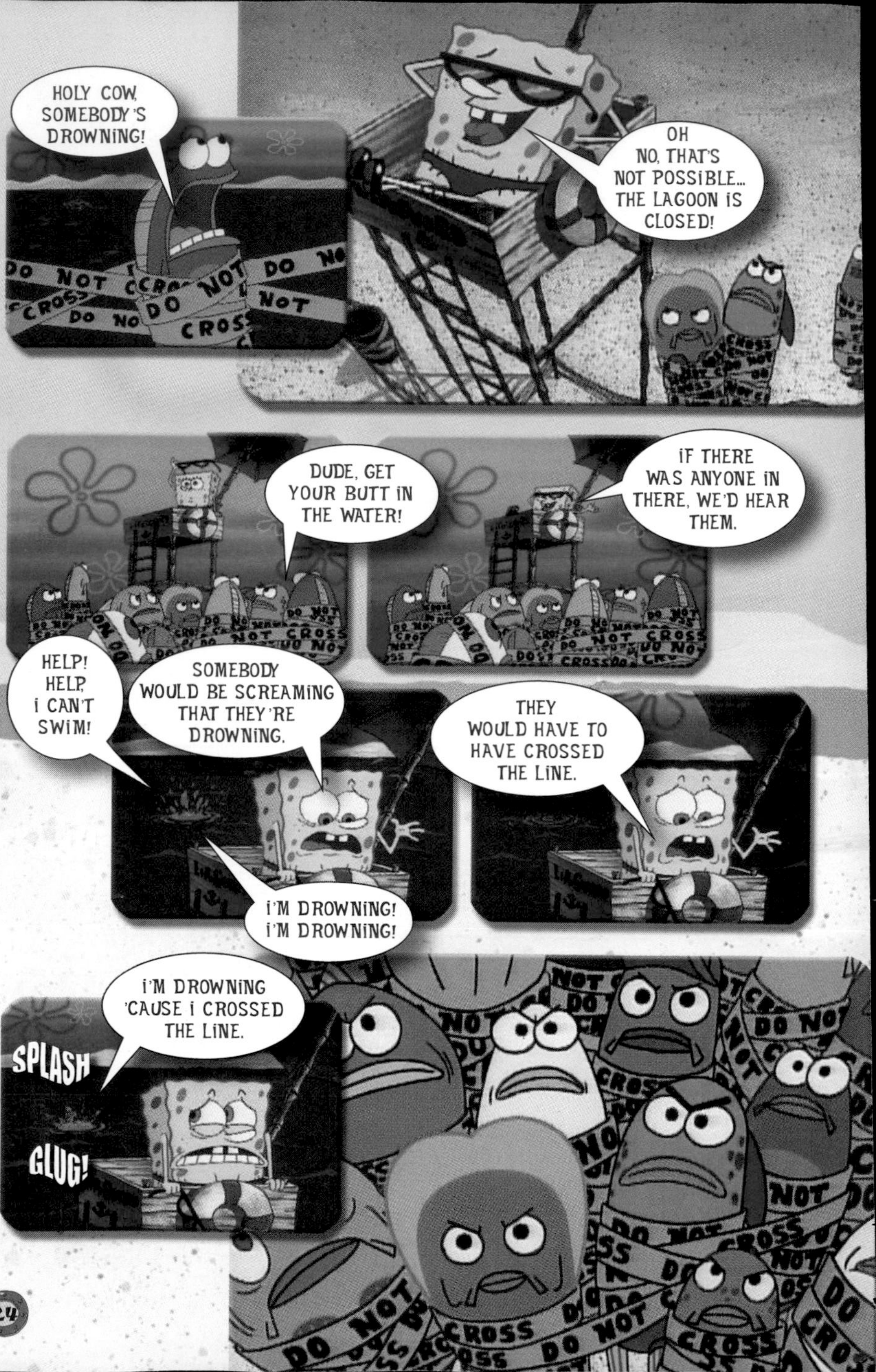
HOLY COW, SOMEBODY'S DROWNING!
OH NO, THAT'S NOT POSSIBLE... THE LAGOON IS CLOSED!
DUDE, GET YOUR BUTT IN THE WATER!
IF THERE WAS ANYONE IN THERE, WE'D HEAR THEM.
HELP! HELP, I CAN'T SWIM!
SOMEBODY WOULD BE SCREAMING THAT THEY'RE DROWNING.
I'M DROWNING! I'M DROWNING!
THEY WOULD HAVE TO HAVE CROSSED THE LINE.
I'M DROWNING 'CAUSE I CROSSED THE LINE.
SPLASH
GLUG!

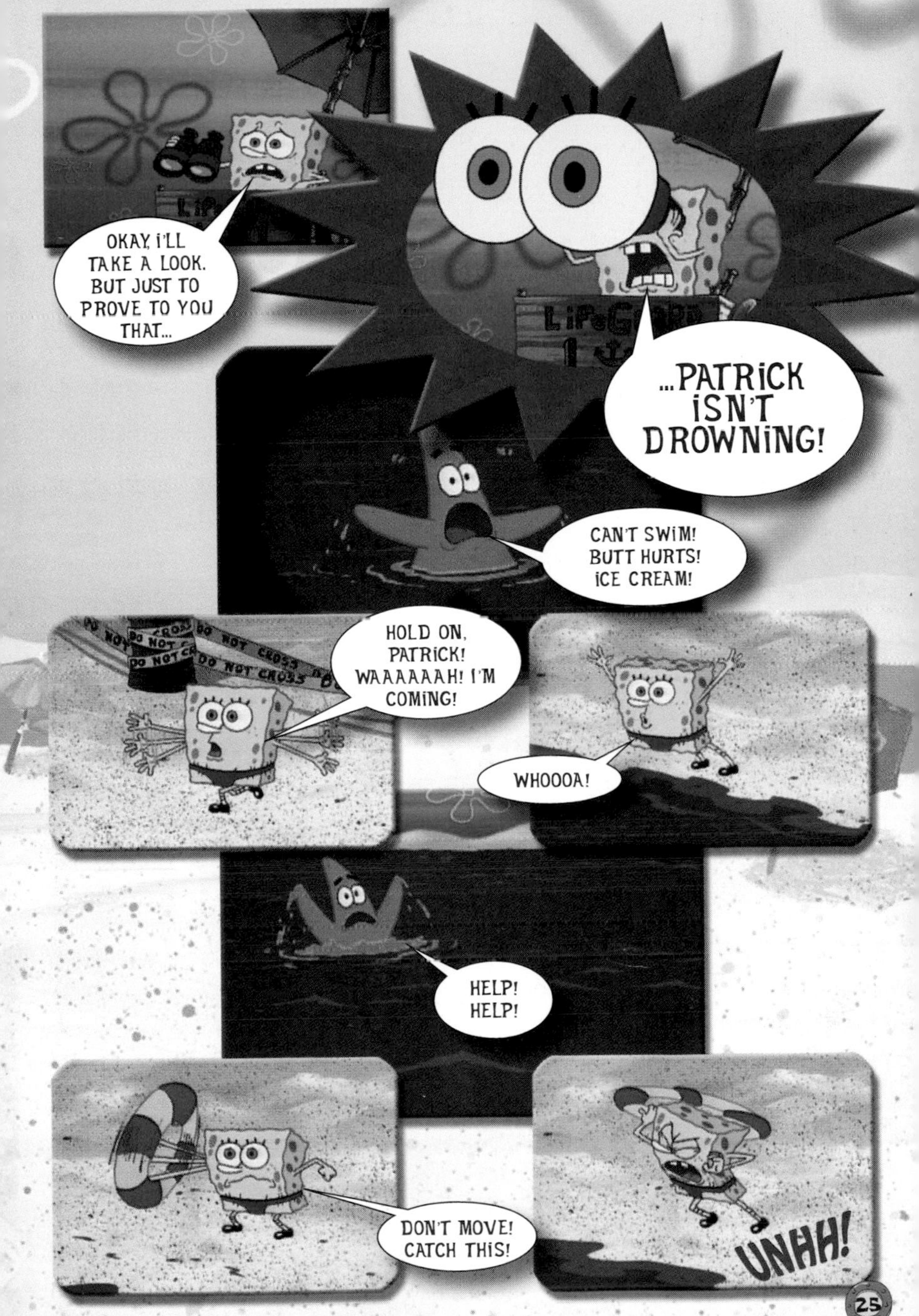
OKAY, I'LL TAKE A LOOK. BUT JUST TO PROVE TO YOU THAT...
...PATRICK ISN'T DROWNING!
CAN'T SWIM! BUTT HURTS! ICE CREAM!
HOLD ON, PATRICK! WAAAAAAH! I'M COMING!
WHOOOA!
HELP! HELP!
DON'T MOVE! CATCH THIS!
UNHH!

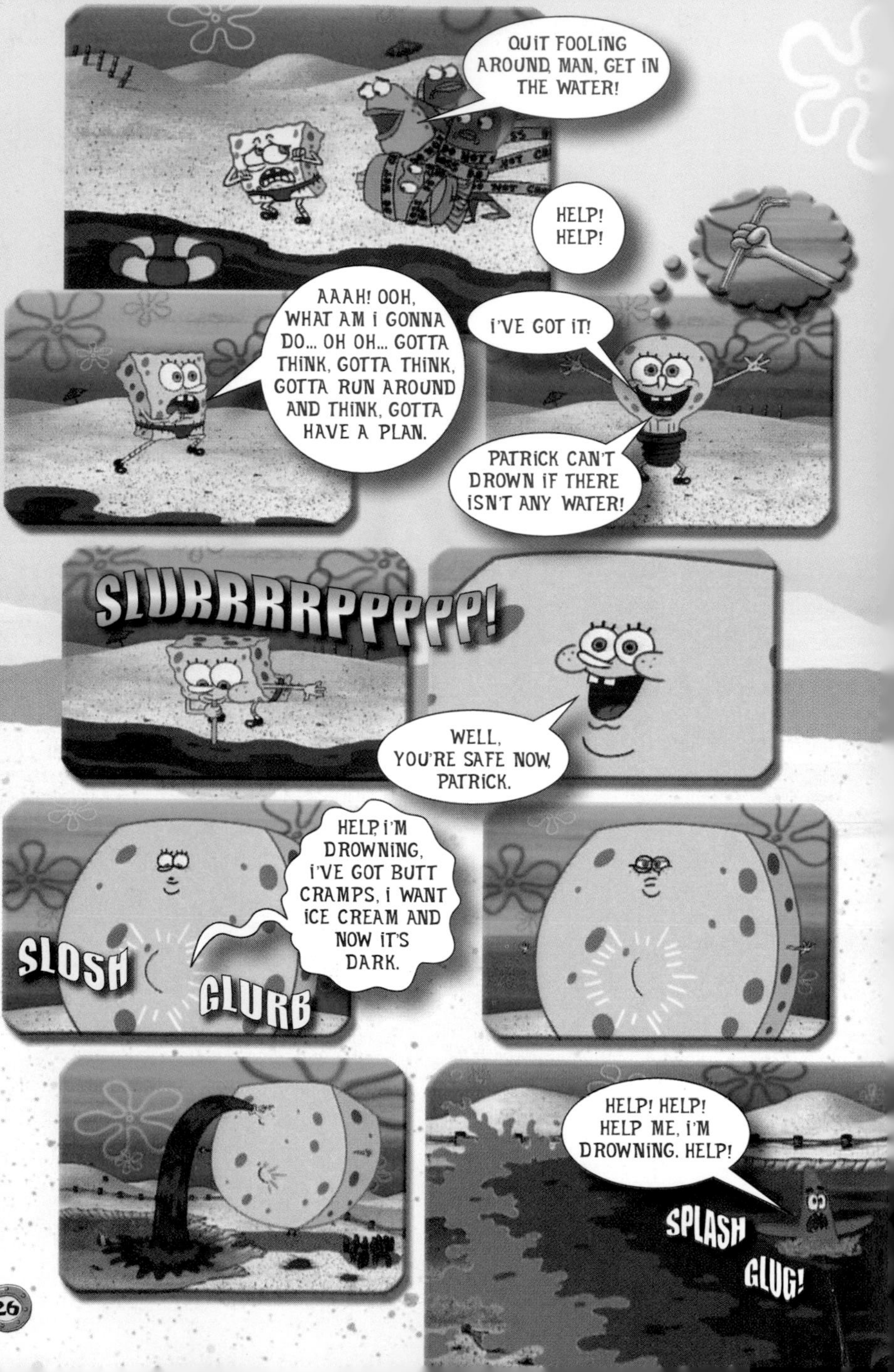

QUIT FOOLING AROUND, MAN, GET IN THE WATER!
HELP! HELP!
AAAH! OOH, WHAT AM I GONNA DO... OH OH... GOTTA THINK, GOTTA THINK, GOTTA RUN AROUND AND THINK, GOTTA HAVE A PLAN.
I'VE GOT IT!
PATRICK CAN'T DROWN IF THERE ISN'T ANY WATER!
SLURRRRRPPPPPP!
WELL, YOU'RE SAFE NOW, PATRICK.
SLOSH
GLURB
HELP, I'M DROWNING, I'VE GOT BUTT CRAMPS, I WANT ICE CREAM AND NOW IT'S DARK.
HELP! HELP! HELP ME, I'M DROWNING. HELP!
SPLASH
GLUG!

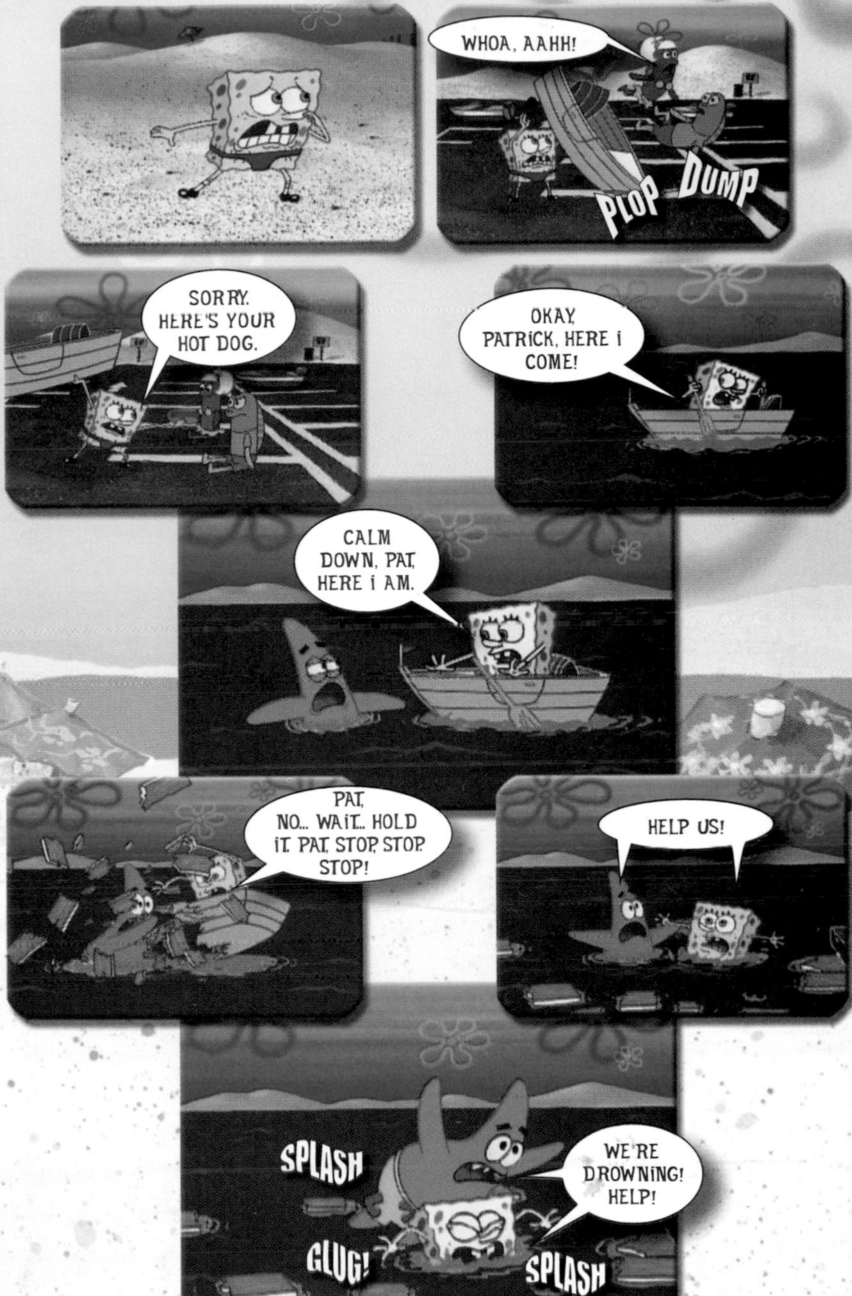
WHOA, AAHH!
PLOP
DUMP
SORRY. HERE'S YOUR HOT DOG.
OKAY, PATRICK, HERE I COME!
CALM DOWN, PAT, HERE I AM.
PAT, NO... WAIT... HOLD IT. PAT, STOP, STOP, STOP!
HELP US!
SPLASH
WE'RE DROWNING! HELP!
GLUG!
SPLASH

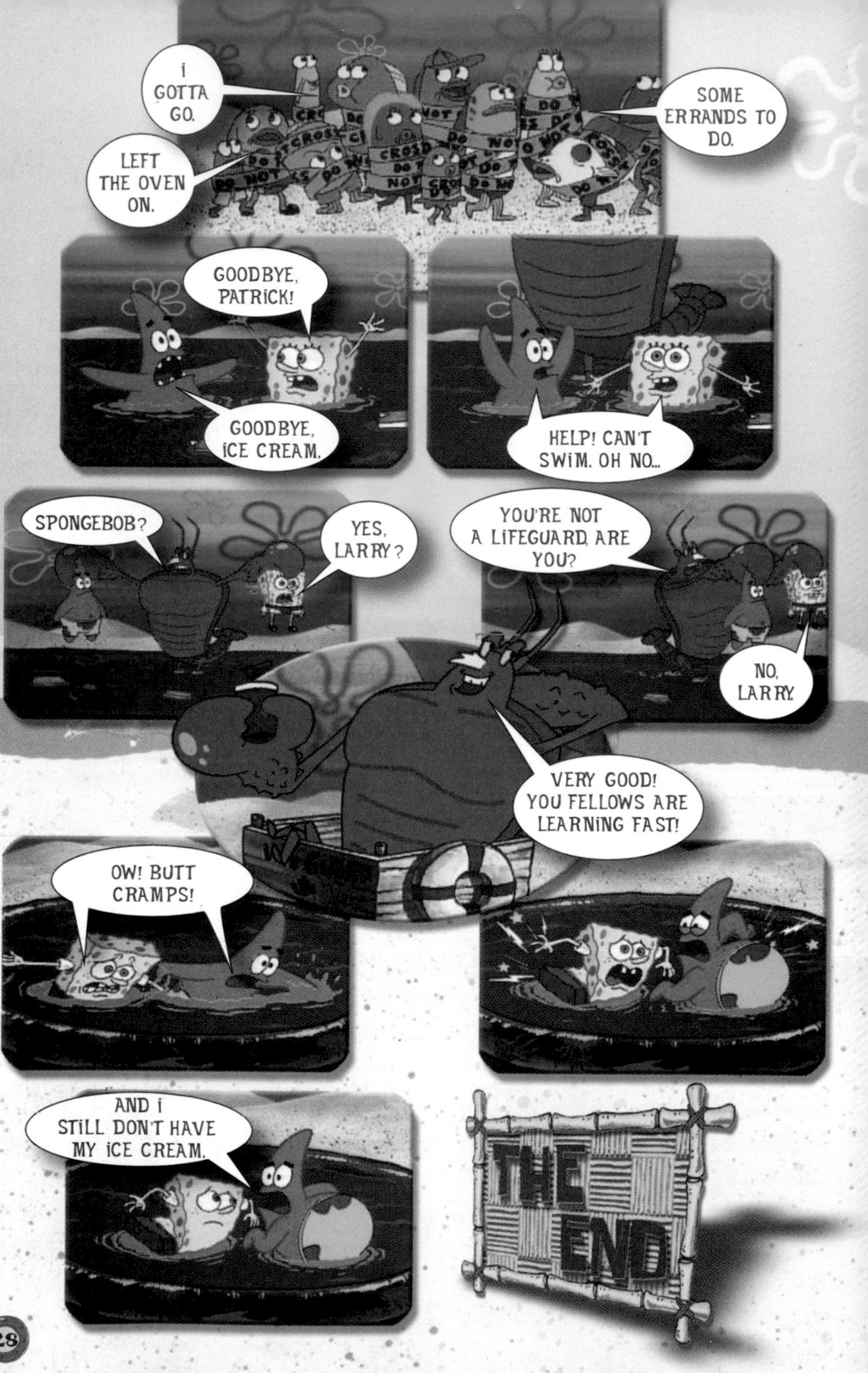
I GOTTA GO.
LEFT THE OVEN ON.
SOME ERRANDS TO DO.
GOODBYE, PATRICK!
GOODBYE, ICE CREAM.
HELP! CAN'T SWIM. OH NO...
SPONGEBOB?
YES, LARRY?
YOU'RE NOT A LIFEGUARD, ARE YOU?
NO, LARRY.
VERY GOOD! YOU FELLOWS ARE LEARNING FAST!
OW! BUTT CRAMPS!
AND I STILL DON'T HAVE MY ICE CREAM.
THE END

SpongeBob SquarePants

Mermaidman and Barnacleboy

by Jay Lender, Sam Henderson and Mark O'Hare

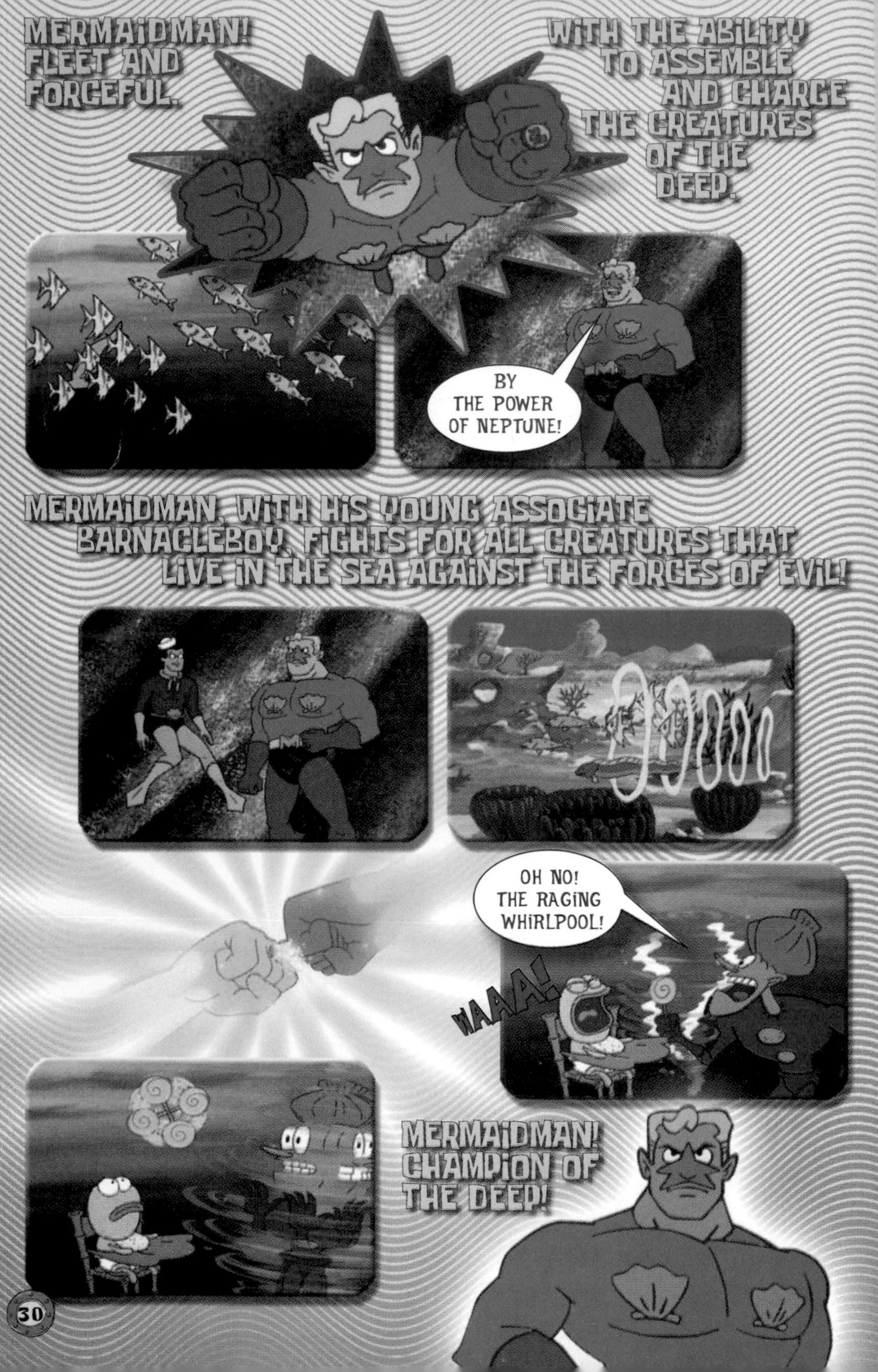
MERMAIDMAN! FLEET AND FORCEFUL.
WITH THE ABILITY TO ASSEMBLE AND CHARGE THE CREATURES OF THE DEEP.
BY THE POWER OF NEPTUNE!
MERMAIDMAN, WITH HIS YOUNG ASSOCIATE BARNACLEBOY, FIGHTS FOR ALL CREATURES THAT LIVE IN THE SEA AGAINST THE FORCES OF EVIL!
WAAA!
OH NO! THE RAGING WHIRLPOOL!
MERMAIDMAN! CHAMPION OF THE DEEP!

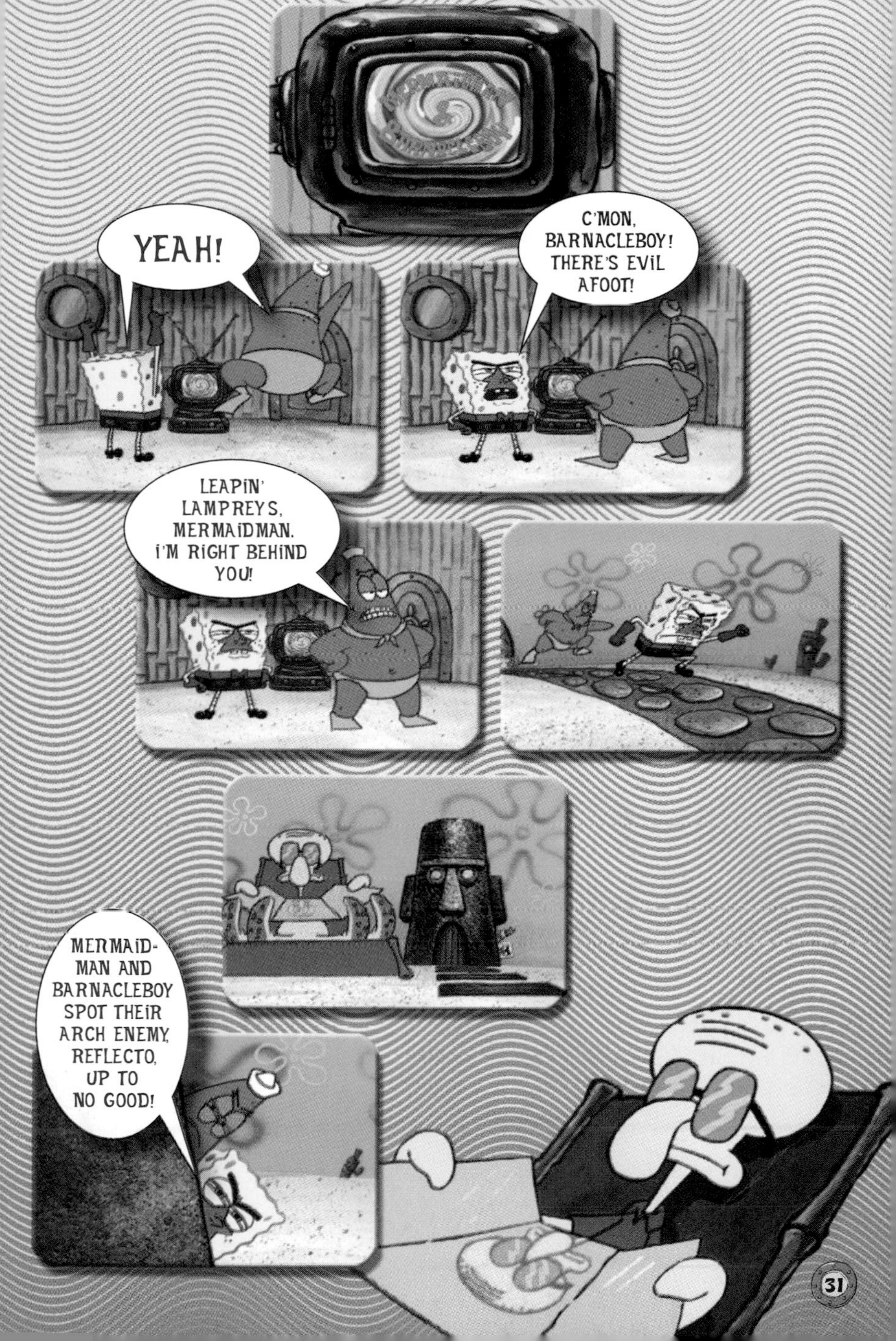
YEAH!
C'MON, BARNACLEBOY! THERE'S EVIL AFOOT!
LEAPIN' LAMPREYS, MERMAIDMAN. I'M RIGHT BEHIND YOU!
MERMAID-MAN AND BARNACLEBOY SPOT THEIR ARCH ENEMY, REFLECTO, UP TO NO GOOD!

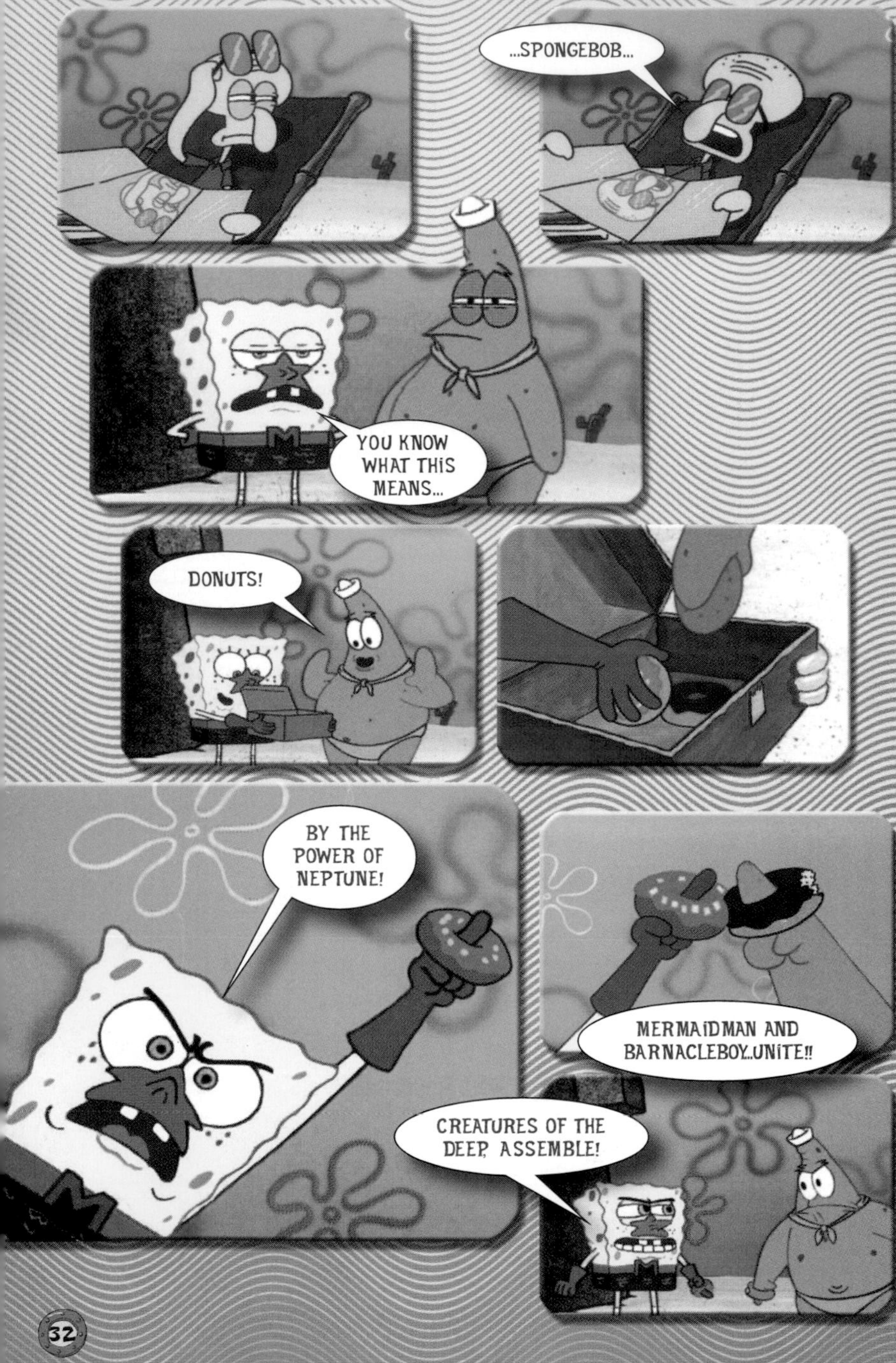
...SPONGEBOB...
YOU KNOW WHAT THIS MEANS...
DONUTS!
BY THE POWER OF NEPTUNE!
MERMAIDMAN AND BARNACLEBOY...UNITE!!
CREATURES OF THE DEEP, ASSEMBLE!

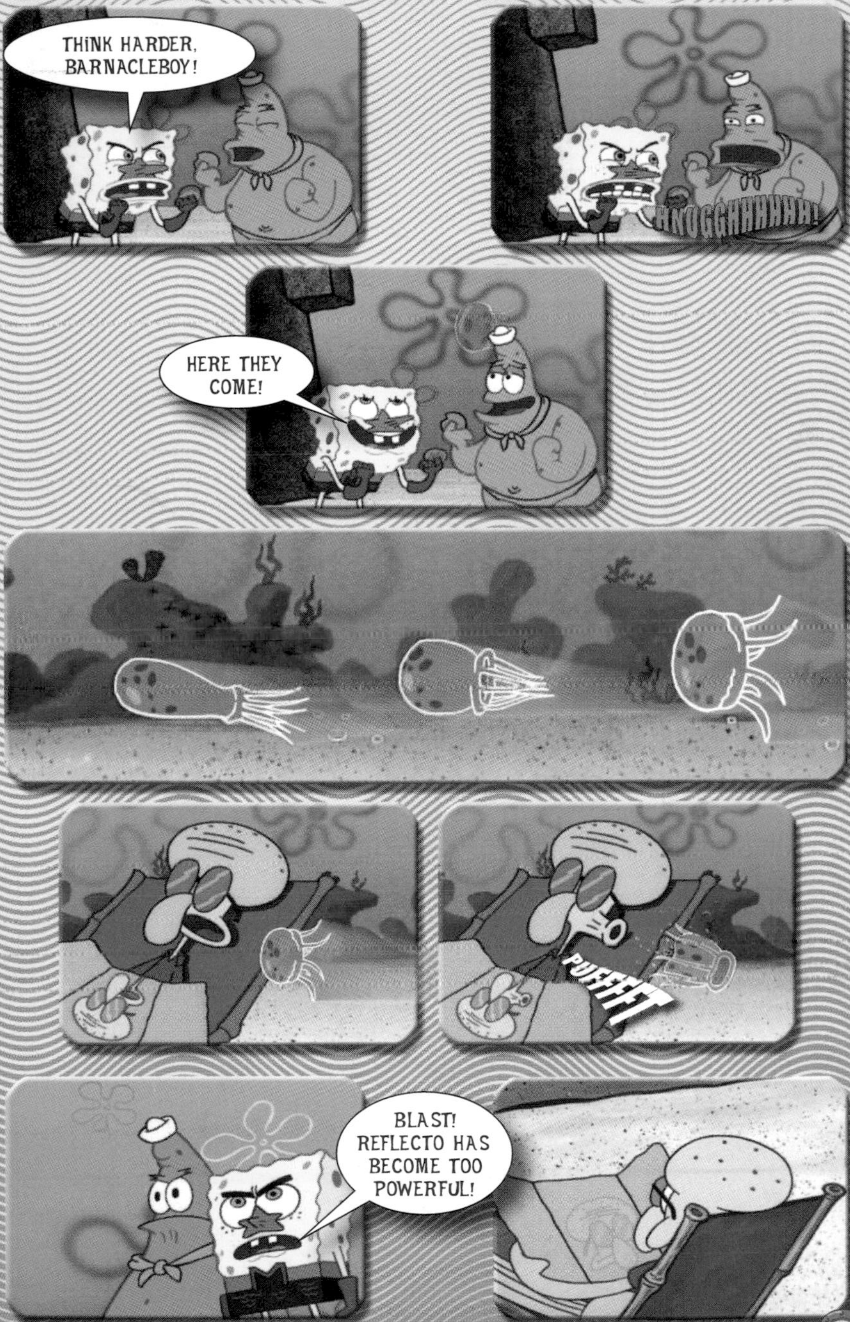
THINK HARDER, BARNACLEBOY!
HNUGGHHHHHH!
HERE THEY COME!
PUFFFT
BLAST! REFLECTO HAS BECOME TOO POWERFUL!

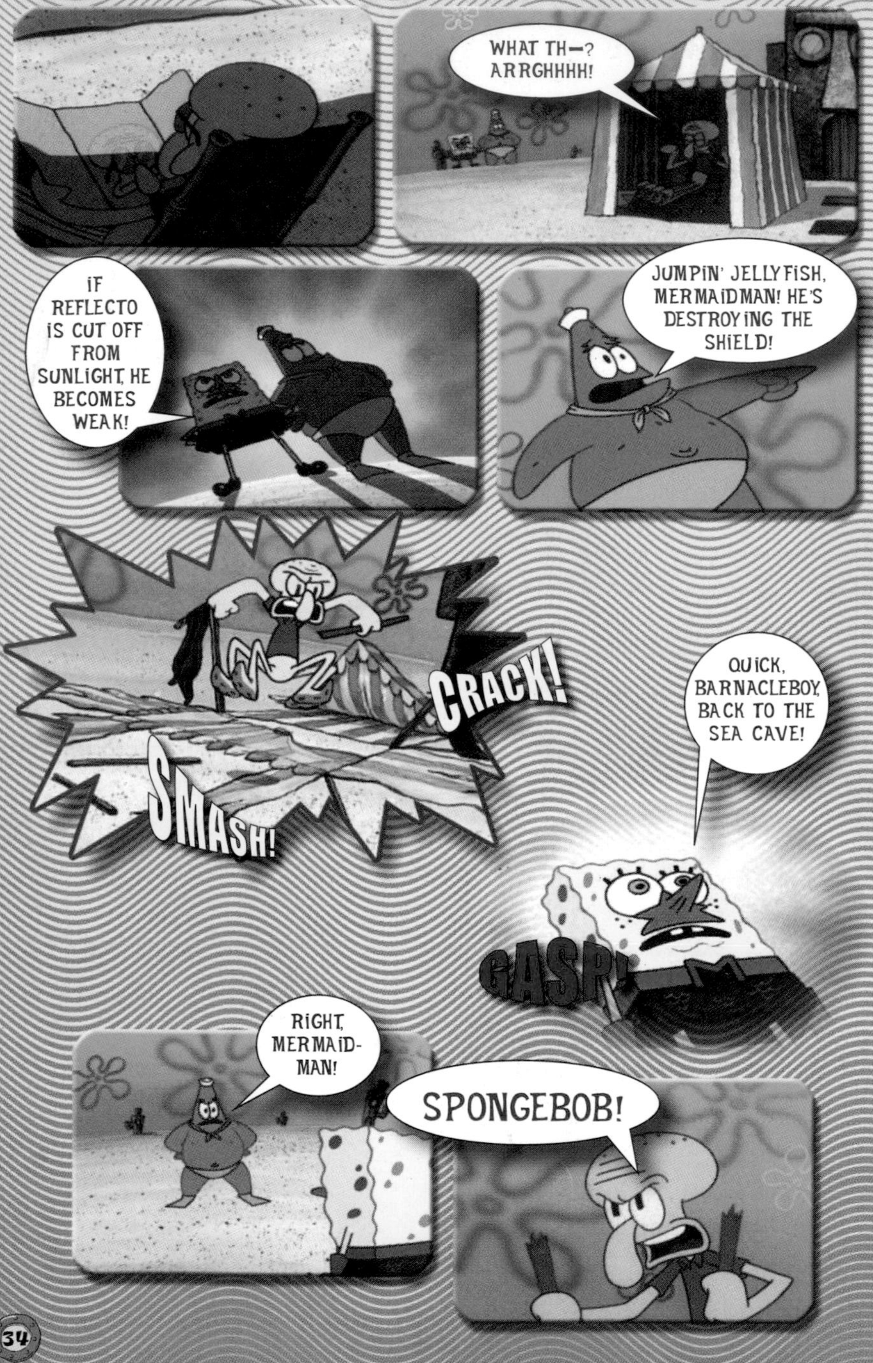
WHAT TH—? ARRGHHHH!
IF REFLECTO IS CUT OFF FROM SUNLIGHT, HE BECOMES WEAK!
JUMPIN' JELLYFISH, MERMAIDMAN! HE'S DESTROYING THE SHIELD!
CRACK!
SMASH!
QUICK, BARNACLEBOY, BACK TO THE SEA CAVE!
GASP!
RIGHT, MERMAID-MAN!
SPONGEBOB!

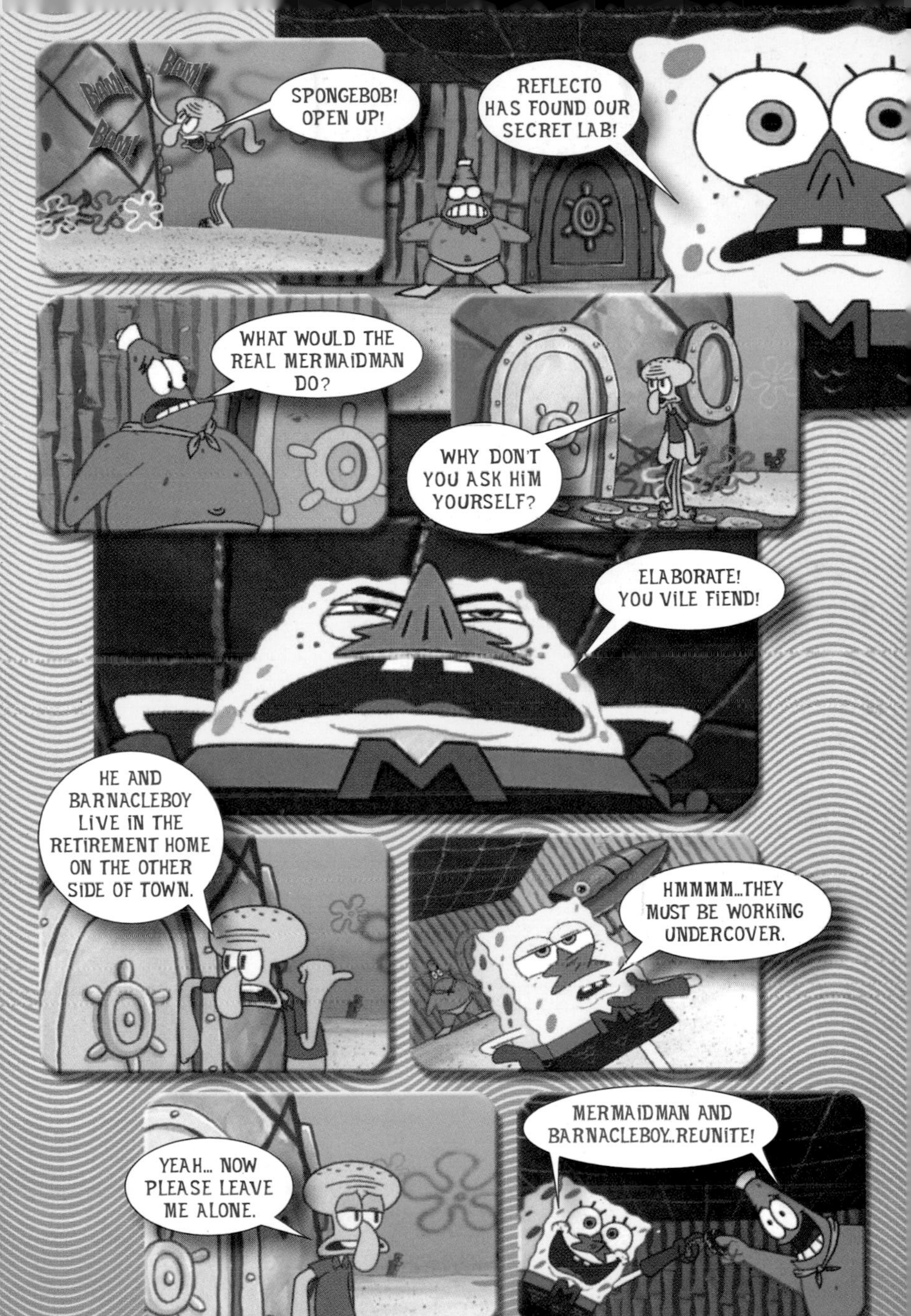
BAM!
BAM!
BAM!
SPONGEBOB! OPEN UP!
REFLECTO HAS FOUND OUR SECRET LAB!
WHAT WOULD THE REAL MERMAIDMAN DO?
WHY DON'T YOU ASK HIM YOURSELF?
ELABORATE! YOU VILE FIEND!
HE AND BARNACLEBOY LIVE IN THE RETIREMENT HOME ON THE OTHER SIDE OF TOWN.
HMMMM...THEY MUST BE WORKING UNDERCOVER.
YEAH... NOW PLEASE LEAVE ME ALONE.
MERMAIDMAN AND BARNACLEBOY...REUNITE!

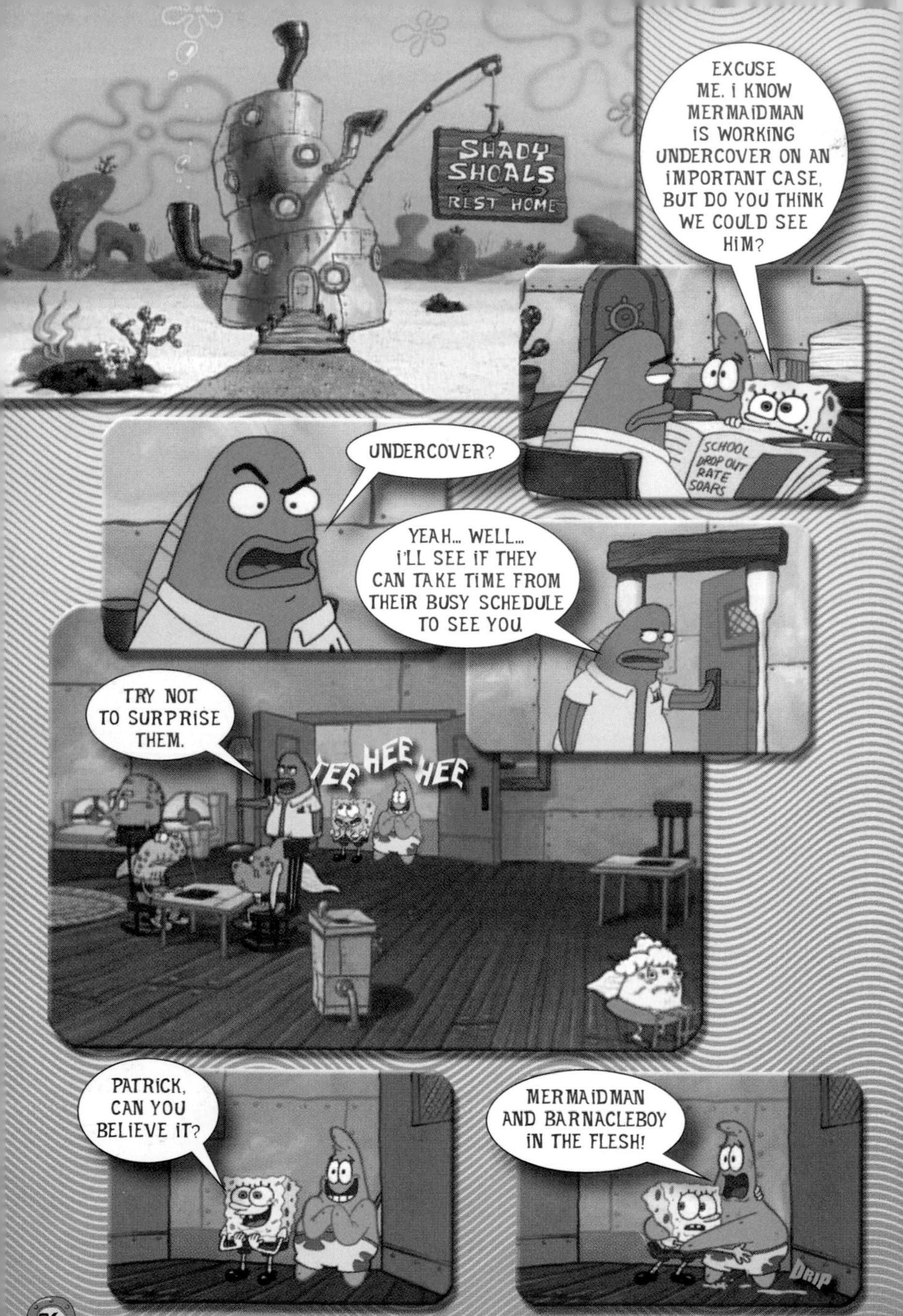
SHADY SHOALS REST HOME
EXCUSE ME. I KNOW MERMAIDMAN IS WORKING UNDERCOVER ON AN IMPORTANT CASE, BUT DO YOU THINK WE COULD SEE HIM?
SCHOOL DROP OUT RATE SOARS
UNDERCOVER?
YEAH... WELL... I'LL SEE IF THEY CAN TAKE TIME FROM THEIR BUSY SCHEDULE TO SEE YOU.
TRY NOT TO SURPRISE THEM.
TEE HEE HEE
PATRICK, CAN YOU BELIEVE IT?
MERMAIDMAN AND BARNACLEBOY IN THE FLESH!
DRIP

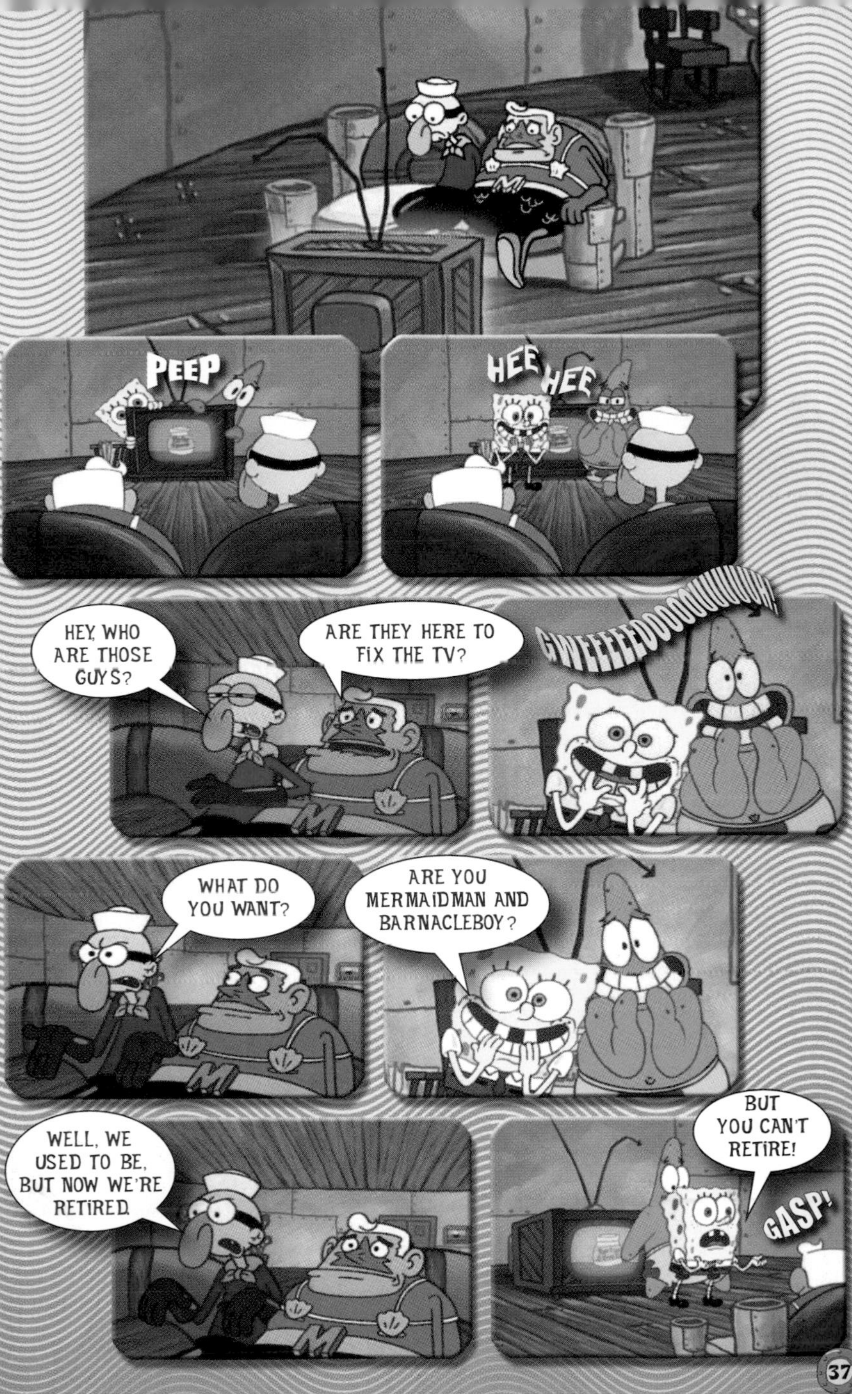
PEEP
HEE HEE
HEY, WHO ARE THOSE GUYS?
ARE THEY HERE TO FIX THE TV?
WHAT DO YOU WANT?
ARE YOU MERMAIDMAN AND BARNACLEBOY?
WELL, WE USED TO BE, BUT NOW WE'RE RETIRED.
BUT YOU CAN'T RETIRE!
GASP!

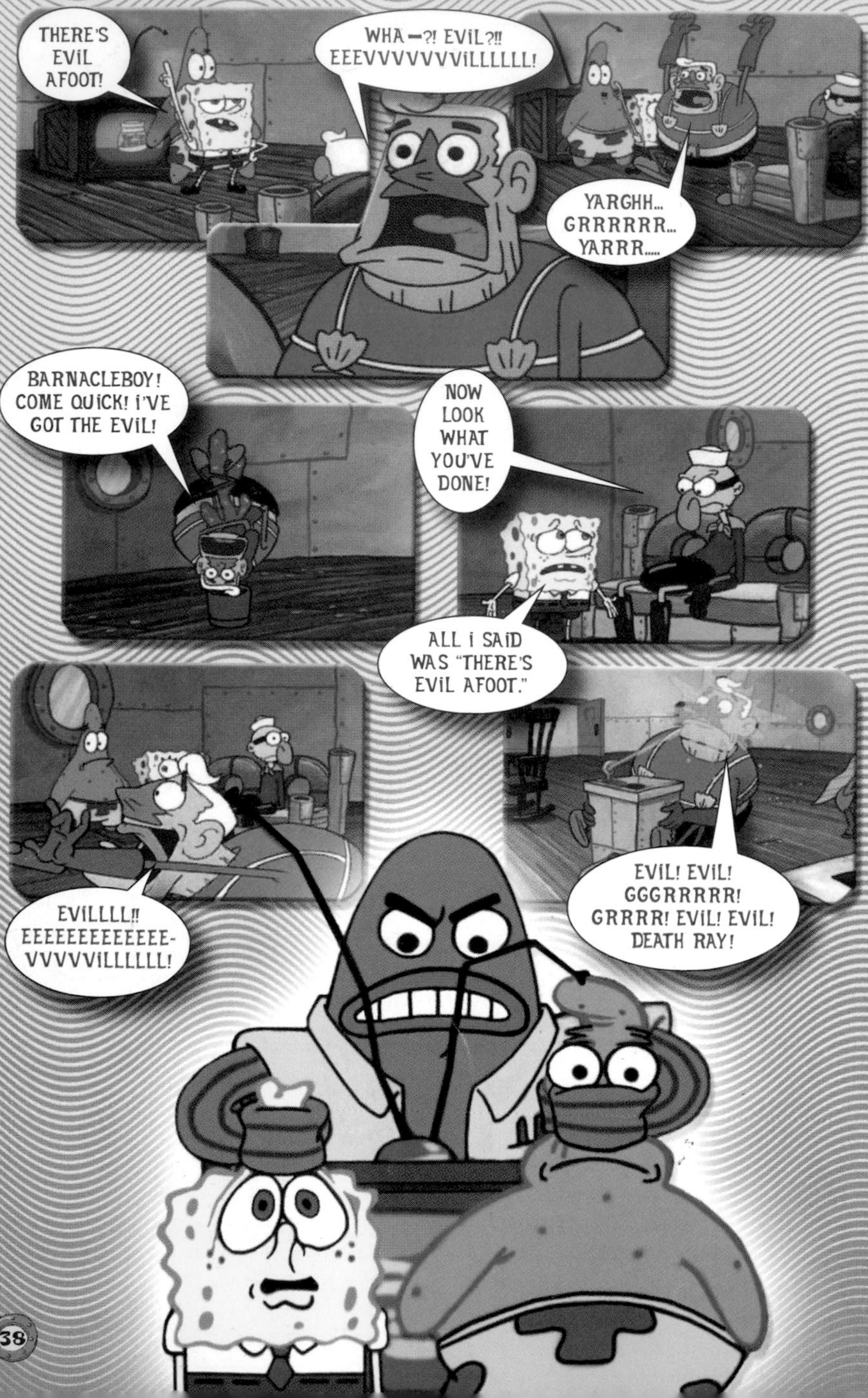
THERE'S EVIL AFOOT!
WHA—?! EVIL?!! EEEVVVVVVVVILLLLLLL!
YARGHH... GRRRRRR... YARRR.....
BARNACLEBOY! COME QUICK! I'VE GOT THE EVIL!
NOW LOOK WHAT YOU'VE DONE!
ALL I SAID WAS "THERE'S EVIL AFOOT."
EVILLLL!! EEEEEEEEEEEE-VVVVVILLLLLLL!
EVIL! EVIL! GGGRRRRR! GRRRR! EVIL! EVIL! DEATH RAY!

WOW! MERMAIDMAN AND BARNACLEBOY!

IT'S TOO BAD THEY'RE OLD.

WHAT DO YOU MEAN, PATRICK? OLD PEOPLE ARE THE GREATEST THEY'RE FULL OF WISDOM AND EXPERIENCE!

THE WORLD NEEDS MERMAIDMAN AND BARNACLEBOY. SOMEONE, SOMEWHERE IS IN TROUBLE!

AND I WON'T REST UNTIL MERMAIDMAN AND BARNACLEBOY ARE OUT OF RETIREMENT!!

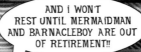

OOOHH... PRETTY LIGHTS.

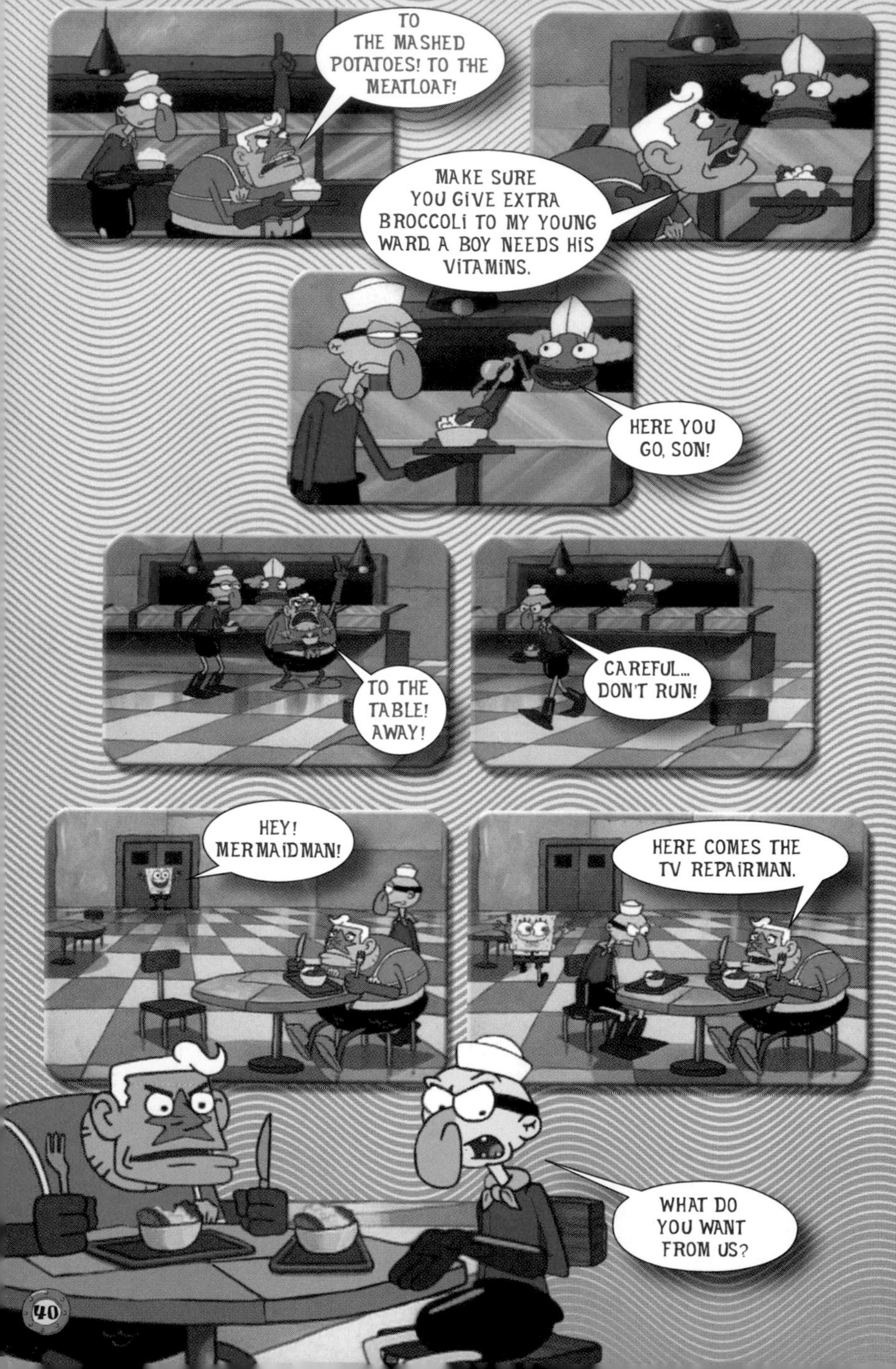
TO THE MASHED POTATOES! TO THE MEATLOAF!
MAKE SURE YOU GIVE EXTRA BROCCOLI TO MY YOUNG WARD. A BOY NEEDS HIS VITAMINS.
HERE YOU GO, SON!
TO THE TABLE! AWAY!
CAREFUL... DON'T RUN!
HEY! MERMAIDMAN!
HERE COMES THE TV REPAIRMAN.
WHAT DO YOU WANT FROM US?

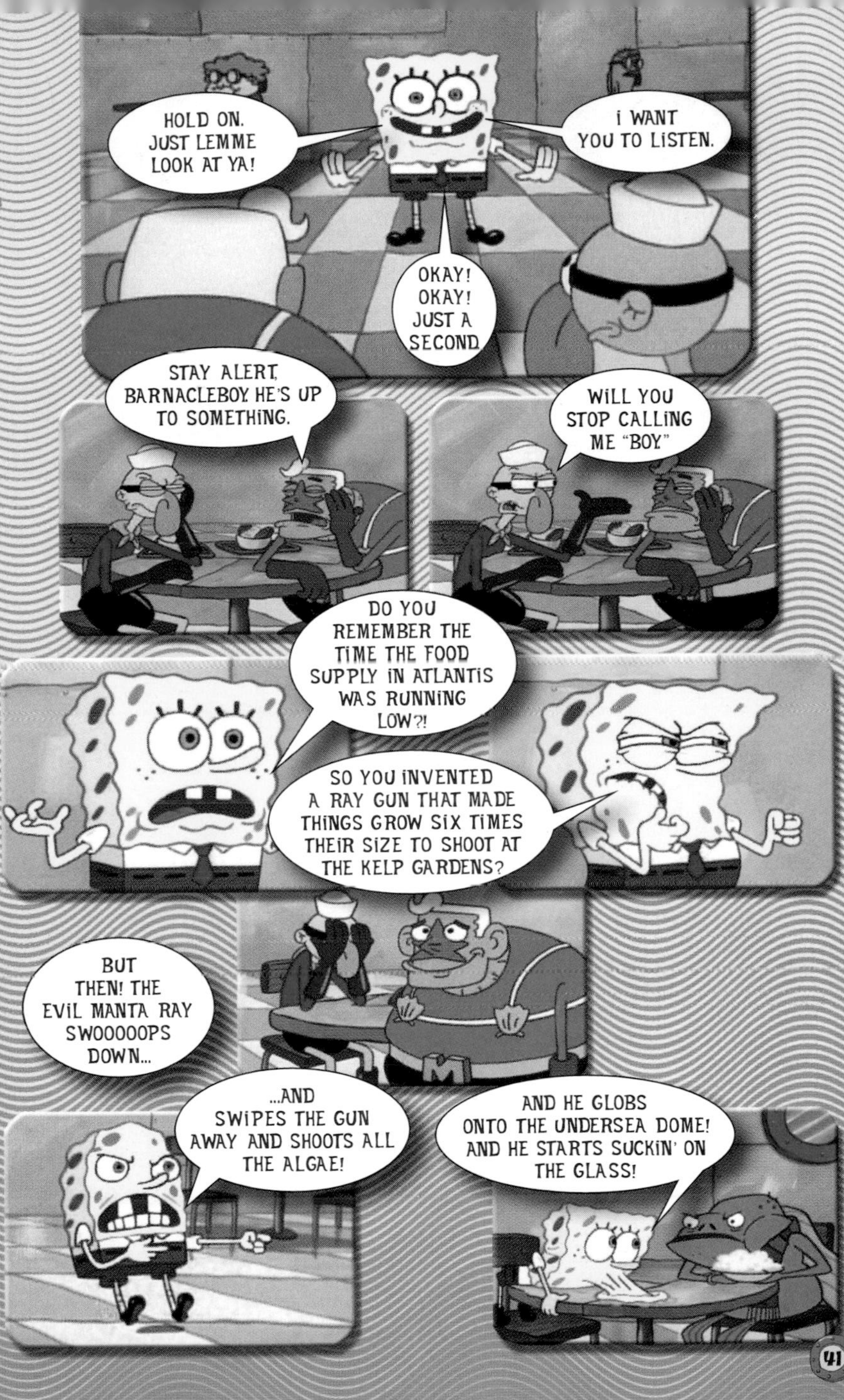
HOLD ON. JUST LEMME LOOK AT YA!
I WANT YOU TO LISTEN.
OKAY! OKAY! JUST A SECOND.
STAY ALERT, BARNACLEBOY. HE'S UP TO SOMETHING.
WILL YOU STOP CALLING ME "BOY."
DO YOU REMEMBER THE TIME THE FOOD SUPPLY IN ATLANTIS WAS RUNNING LOW?!
SO YOU INVENTED A RAY GUN THAT MADE THINGS GROW SIX TIMES THEIR SIZE TO SHOOT AT THE KELP GARDENS?
BUT THEN! THE EVIL MANTA RAY SWOOOOOPS DOWN...
...AND SWIPES THE GUN AWAY AND SHOOTS ALL THE ALGAE!
AND HE GLOBS ONTO THE UNDERSEA DOME! AND HE STARTS SUCKIN' ON THE GLASS!

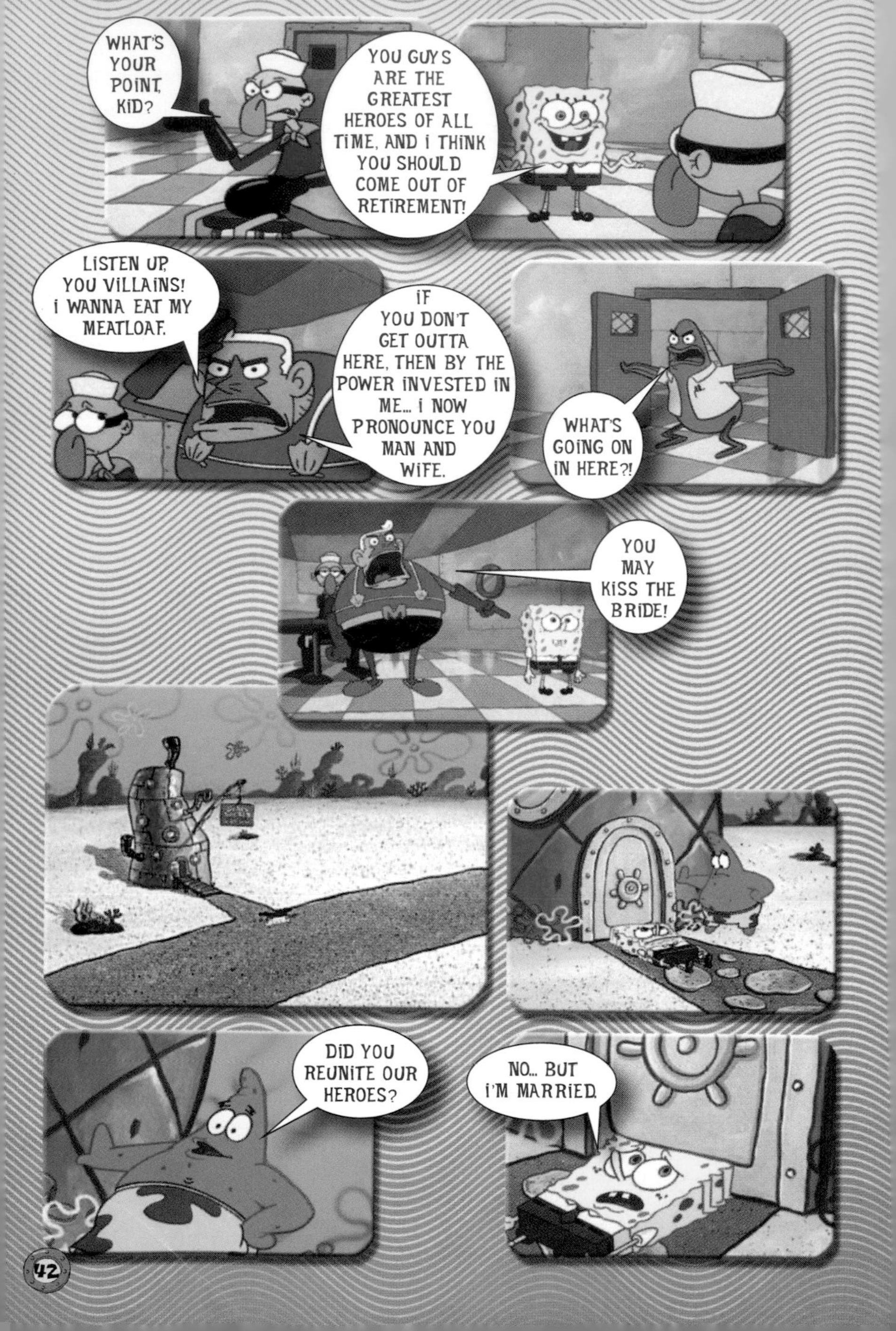
WHAT'S YOUR POINT, KID?
YOU GUYS ARE THE GREATEST HEROES OF ALL TIME, AND I THINK YOU SHOULD COME OUT OF RETIREMENT!
LISTEN UP, YOU VILLAINS! I WANNA EAT MY MEATLOAF.
IF YOU DON'T GET OUTTA HERE, THEN BY THE POWER INVESTED IN ME... I NOW PRONOUNCE YOU MAN AND WIFE.
WHAT'S GOING ON IN HERE?!
YOU MAY KISS THE BRIDE!
DID YOU REUNITE OUR HEROES?
NO... BUT I'M MARRIED.

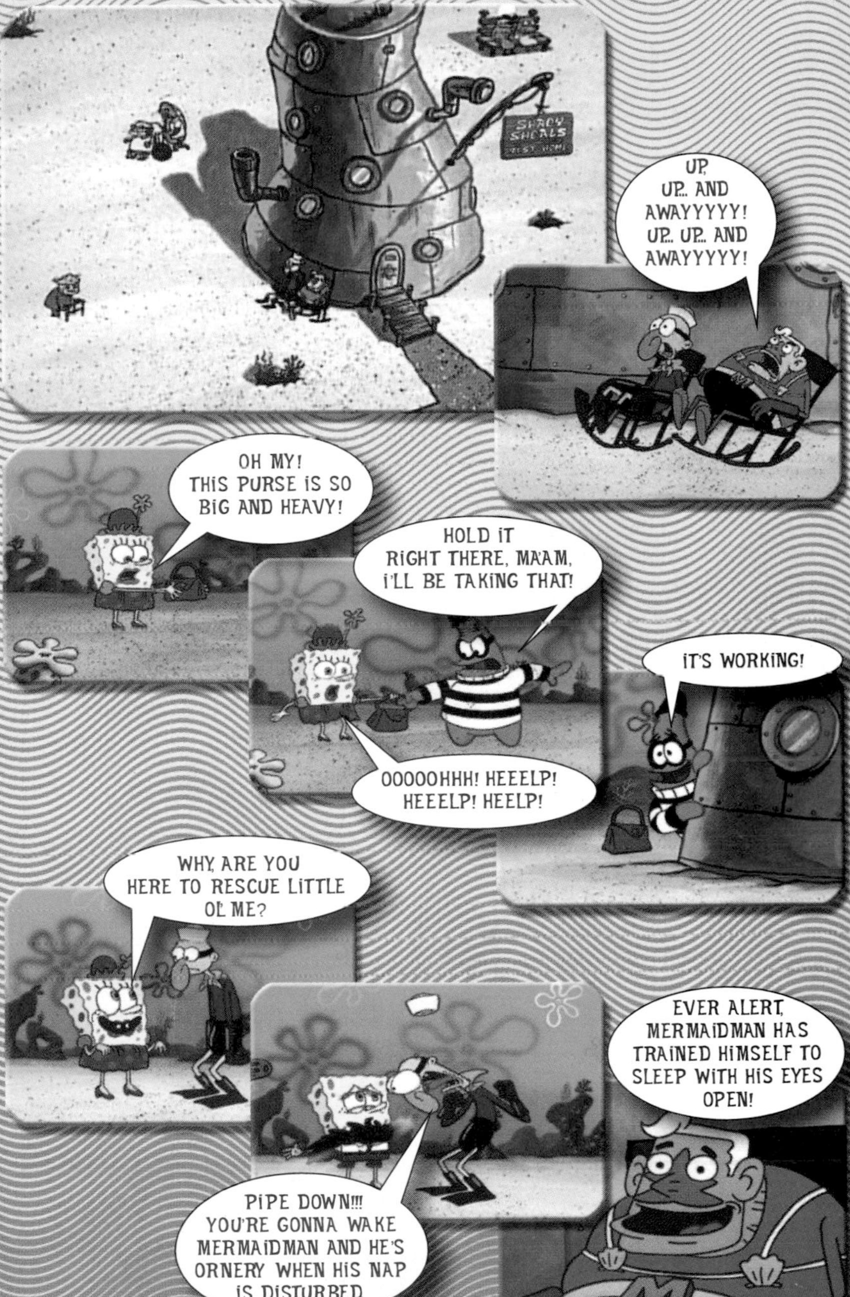
SHADY SHOALS
UP, UP... AND AWAYYYYY! UP... UP... AND AWAYYYYY!
OH MY! THIS PURSE IS SO BIG AND HEAVY!
HOLD IT RIGHT THERE, MA'AM, I'LL BE TAKING THAT!
OOOOOHHH! HEEELP! HEEELP! HEELP!
IT'S WORKING!
WHY, ARE YOU HERE TO RESCUE LITTLE OL' ME?
PIPE DOWN!!! YOU'RE GONNA WAKE MERMAIDMAN AND HE'S ORNERY WHEN HIS NAP IS DISTURBED.
EVER ALERT, MERMAIDMAN HAS TRAINED HIMSELF TO SLEEP WITH HIS EYES OPEN!

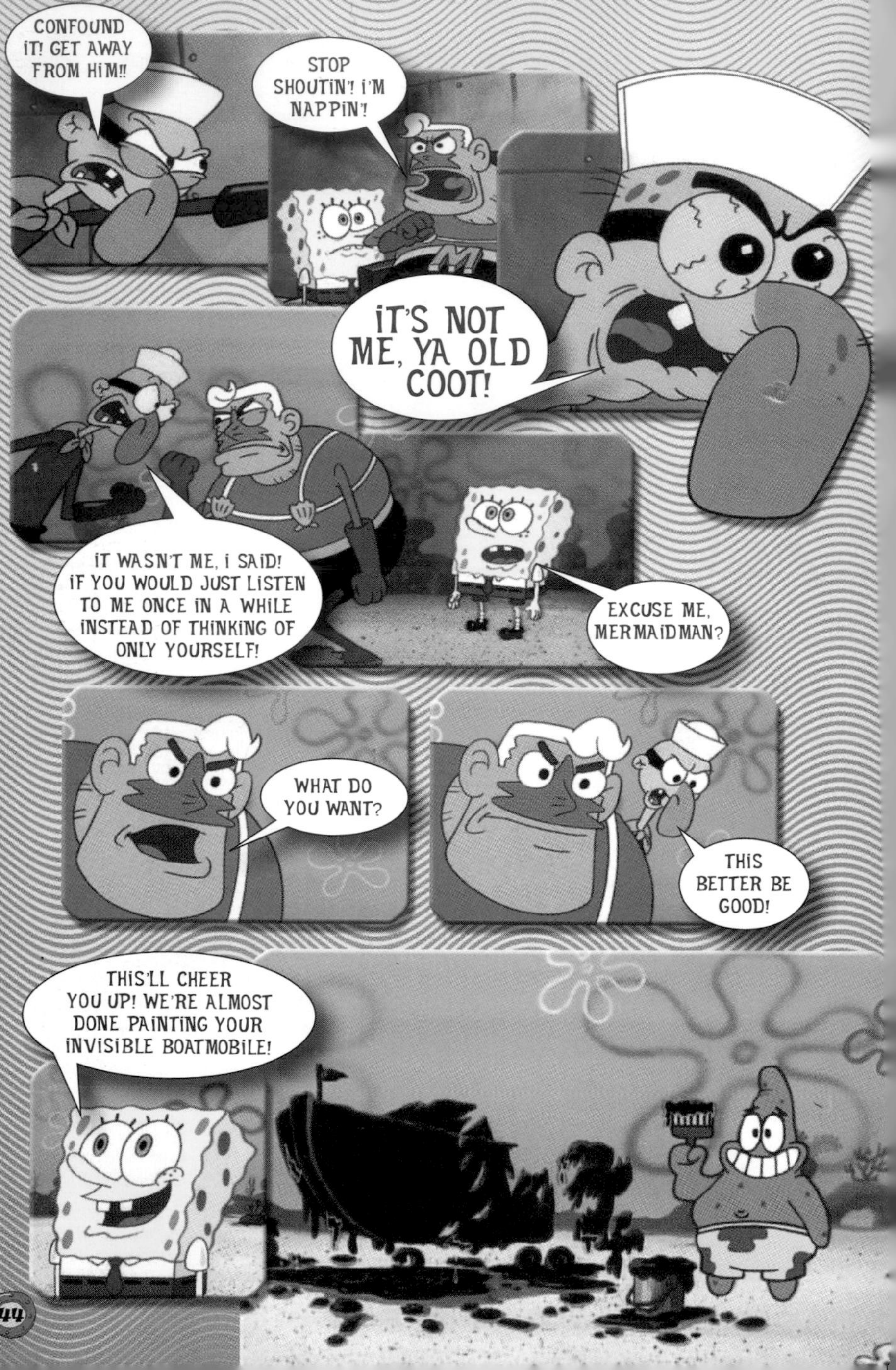

CONFOUND IT! GET AWAY FROM HIM!!
STOP SHOUTIN'! I'M NAPPIN'!
IT'S NOT ME, YA OLD COOT!
IT WASN'T ME, I SAID! IF YOU WOULD JUST LISTEN TO ME ONCE IN A WHILE INSTEAD OF THINKING OF ONLY YOURSELF!
EXCUSE ME, MERMAIDMAN?
WHAT DO YOU WANT?
THIS BETTER BE GOOD!
THIS'LL CHEER YOU UP! WE'RE ALMOST DONE PAINTING YOUR INVISIBLE BOATMOBILE!

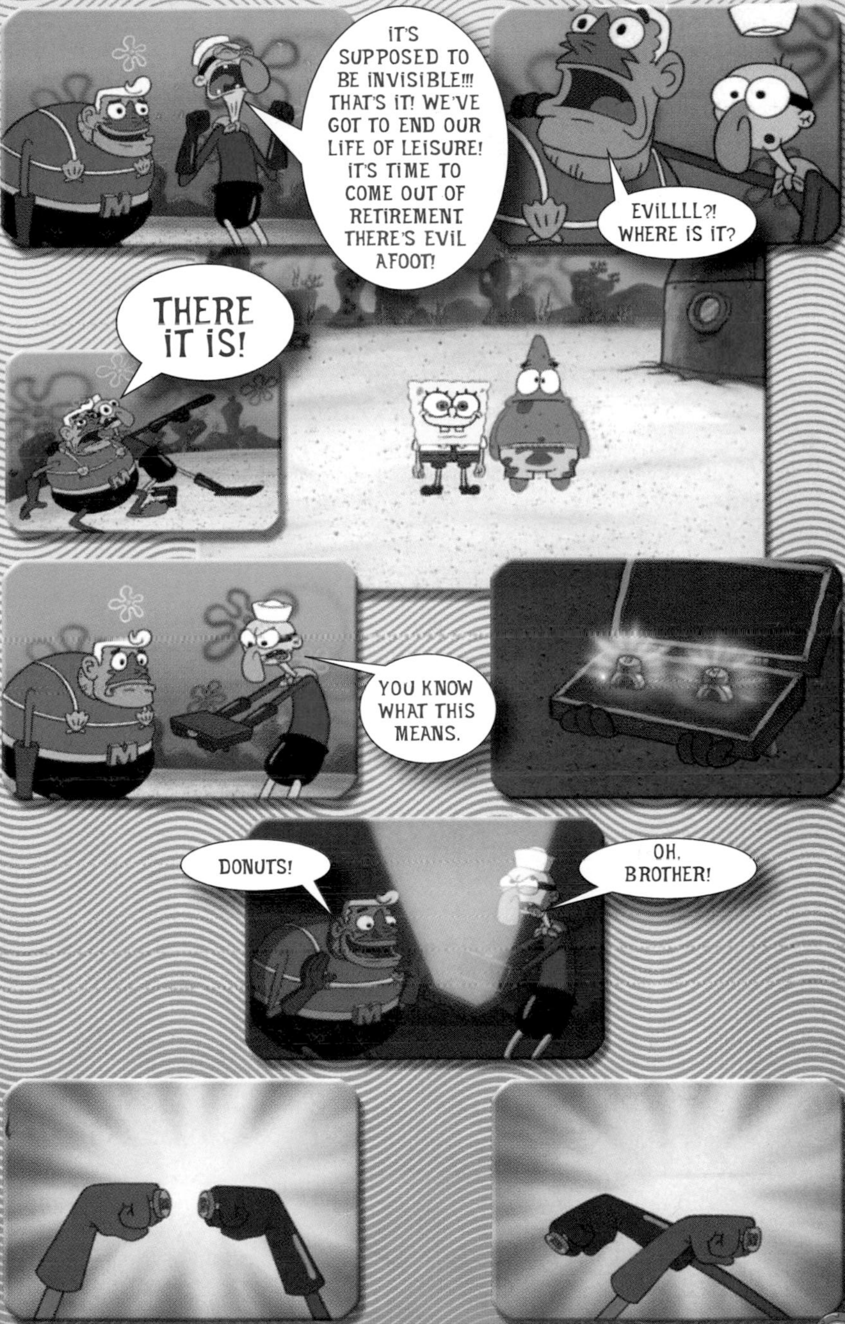
IT'S SUPPOSED TO BE INVISIBLE!!! THAT'S IT! WE'VE GOT TO END OUR LIFE OF LEISURE! IT'S TIME TO COME OUT OF RETIREMENT. THERE'S EVIL AFOOT!
EVILLLL?! WHERE IS IT?
THERE IT IS!
YOU KNOW WHAT THIS MEANS.
DONUTS!
OH, BROTHER!

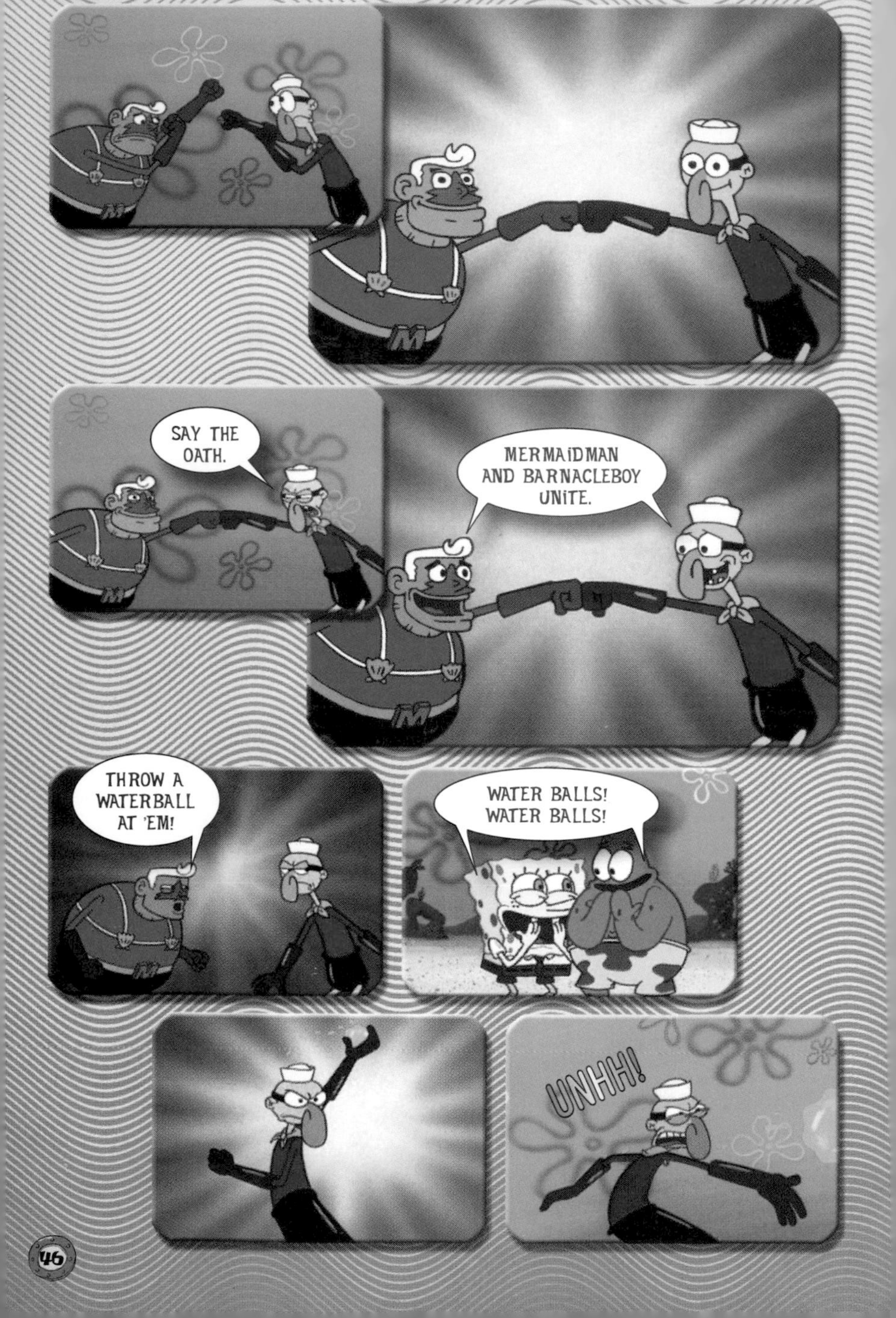
SAY THE OATH.
MERMAIDMAN AND BARNACLEBOY UNITE.
THROW A WATERBALL AT 'EM!
WATER BALLS! WATER BALLS!
UNHH!

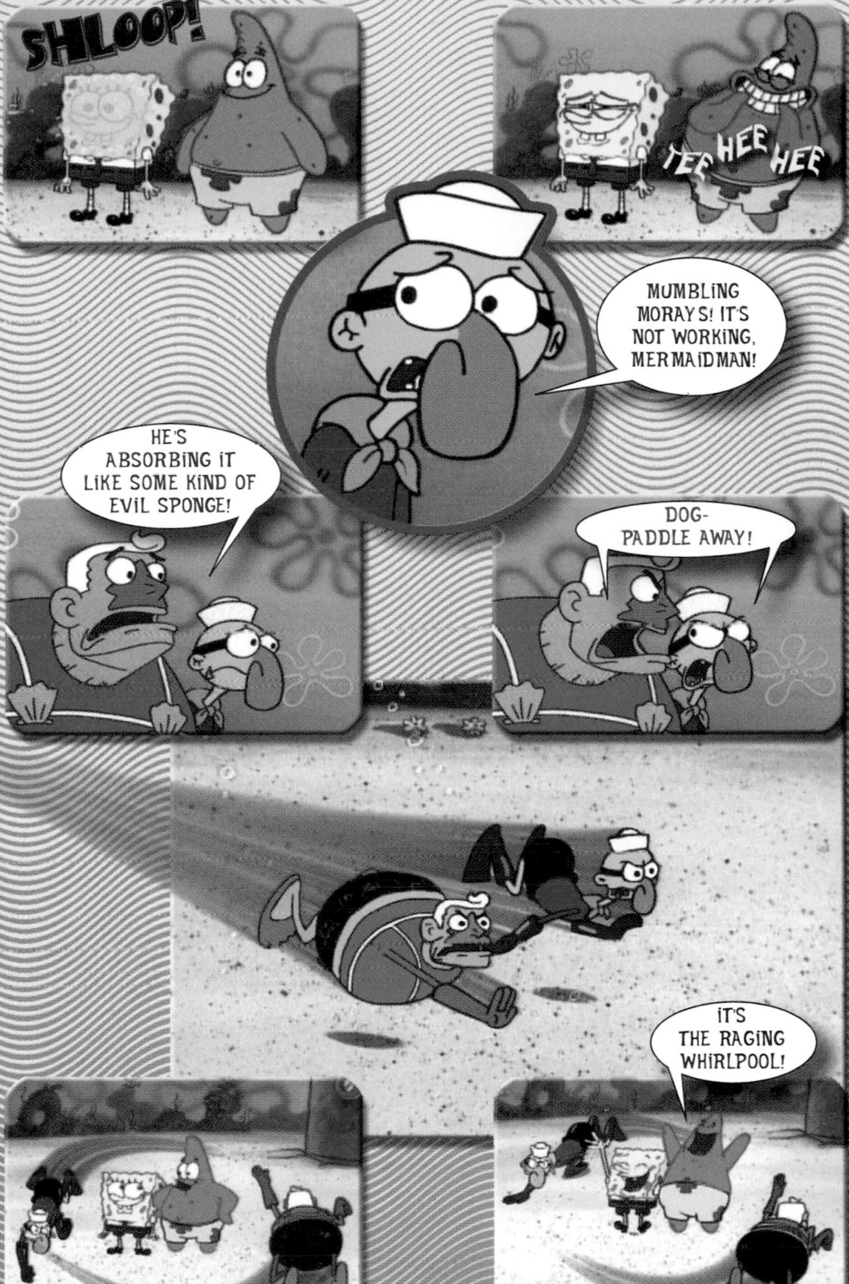
SHLOOP!
TEE HEE HEE
MUMBLING MORAYS! IT'S NOT WORKING, MERMAIDMAN!
HE'S ABSORBING IT LIKE SOME KIND OF EVIL SPONGE!
DOG-PADDLE AWAY!
IT'S THE RAGING WHIRLPOOL!

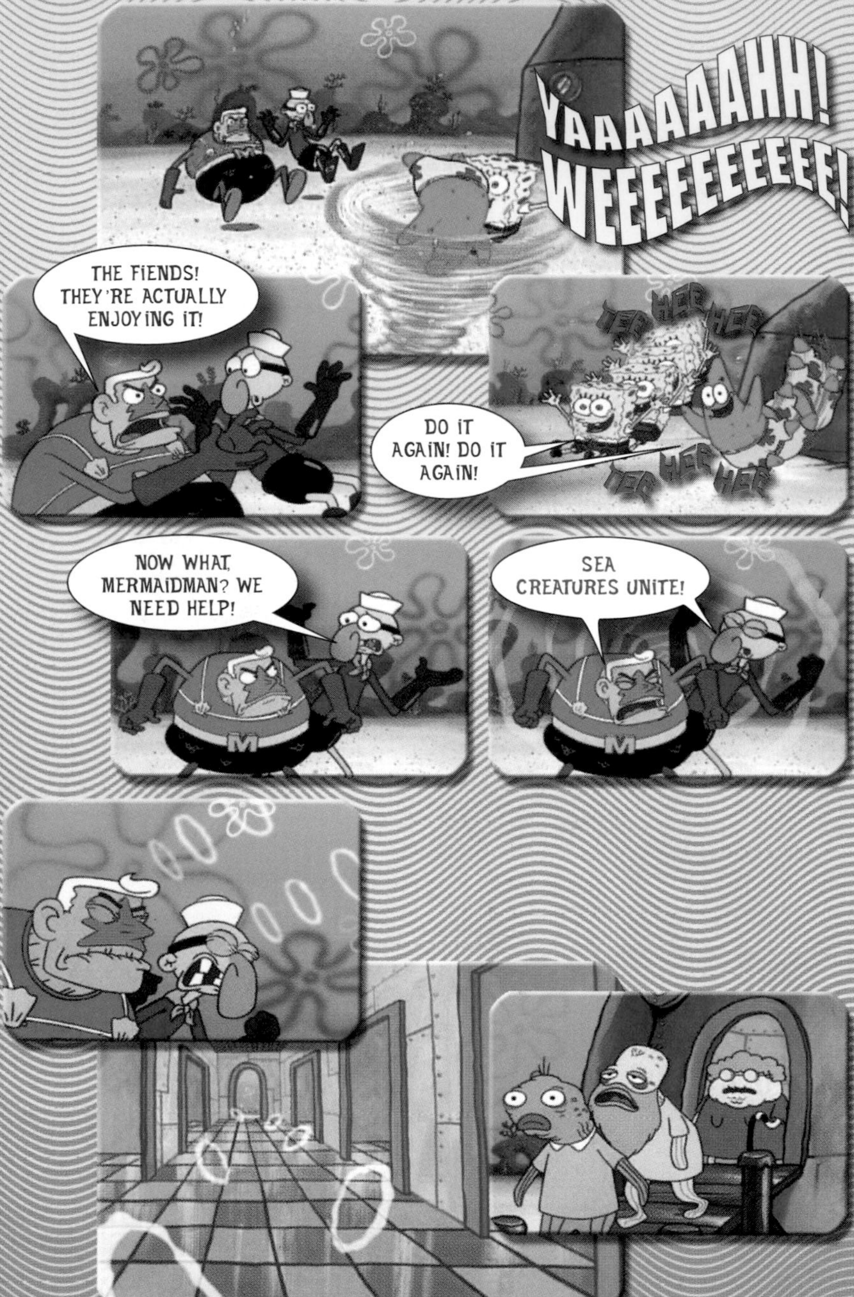
YAAAAAAHH!
WEEEEEEEEEE!
THE FIENDS! THEY'RE ACTUALLY ENJOYING IT!
DO IT AGAIN! DO IT AGAIN!
HEE HEE HEE
HEE HEE HEE
NOW WHAT, MERMAIDMAN? WE NEED HELP!
SEA CREATURES UNITE!

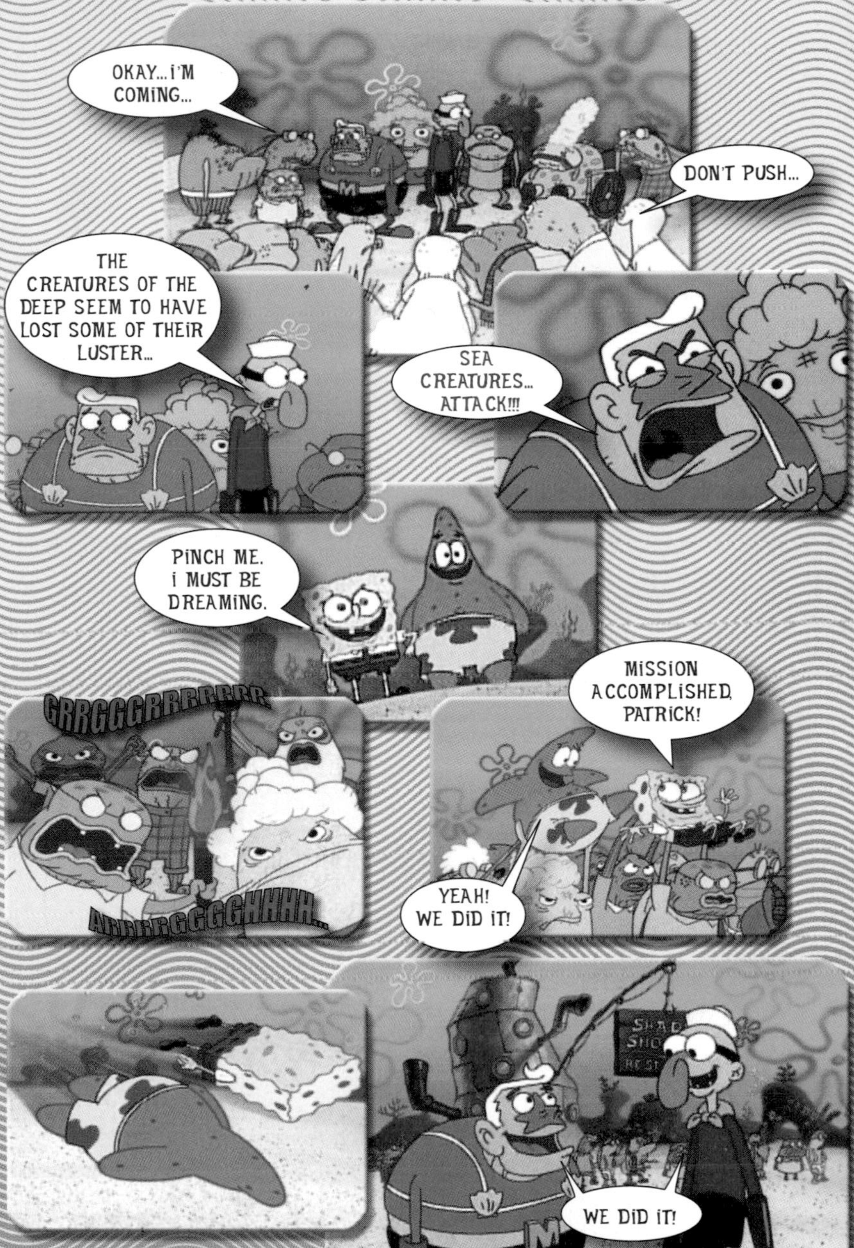
OKAY...I'M COMING...
DON'T PUSH...
THE CREATURES OF THE DEEP SEEM TO HAVE LOST SOME OF THEIR LUSTER...
SEA CREATURES... ATTACK!!!
PINCH ME. I MUST BE DREAMING.
GRRGGGRRRRRRRR.
ARRRRGGGGHHHH...
MISSION ACCOMPLISHED, PATRICK!
YEAH! WE DID IT!
WE DID IT!

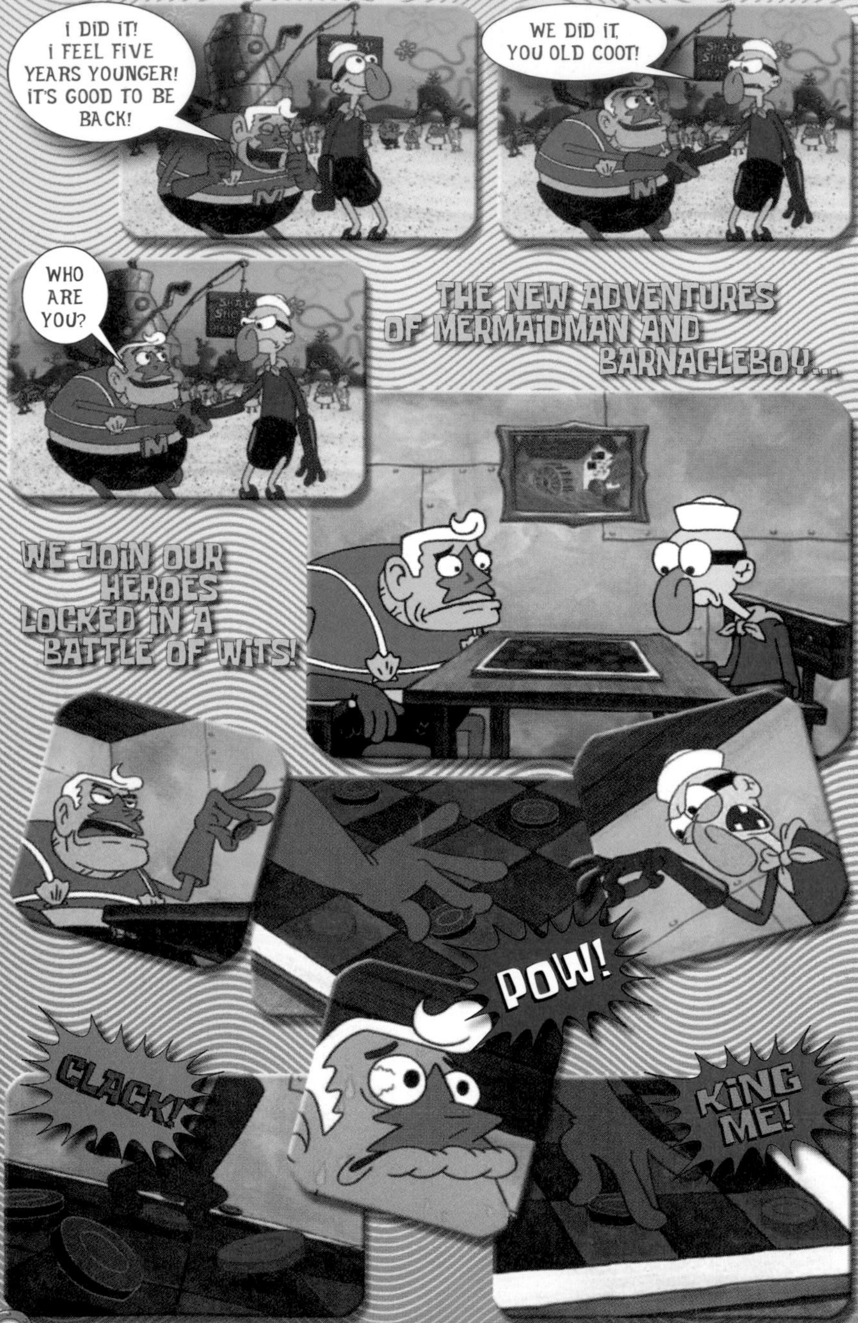
I DID IT! I FEEL FIVE YEARS YOUNGER! IT'S GOOD TO BE BACK!
WE DID IT, YOU OLD COOT!
WHO ARE YOU?
THE NEW ADVENTURES OF MERMAIDMAN AND BARNACLEBOY...
WE JOIN OUR HEROES LOCKED IN A BATTLE OF WITS!
POW!
CLACK!
KING ME!

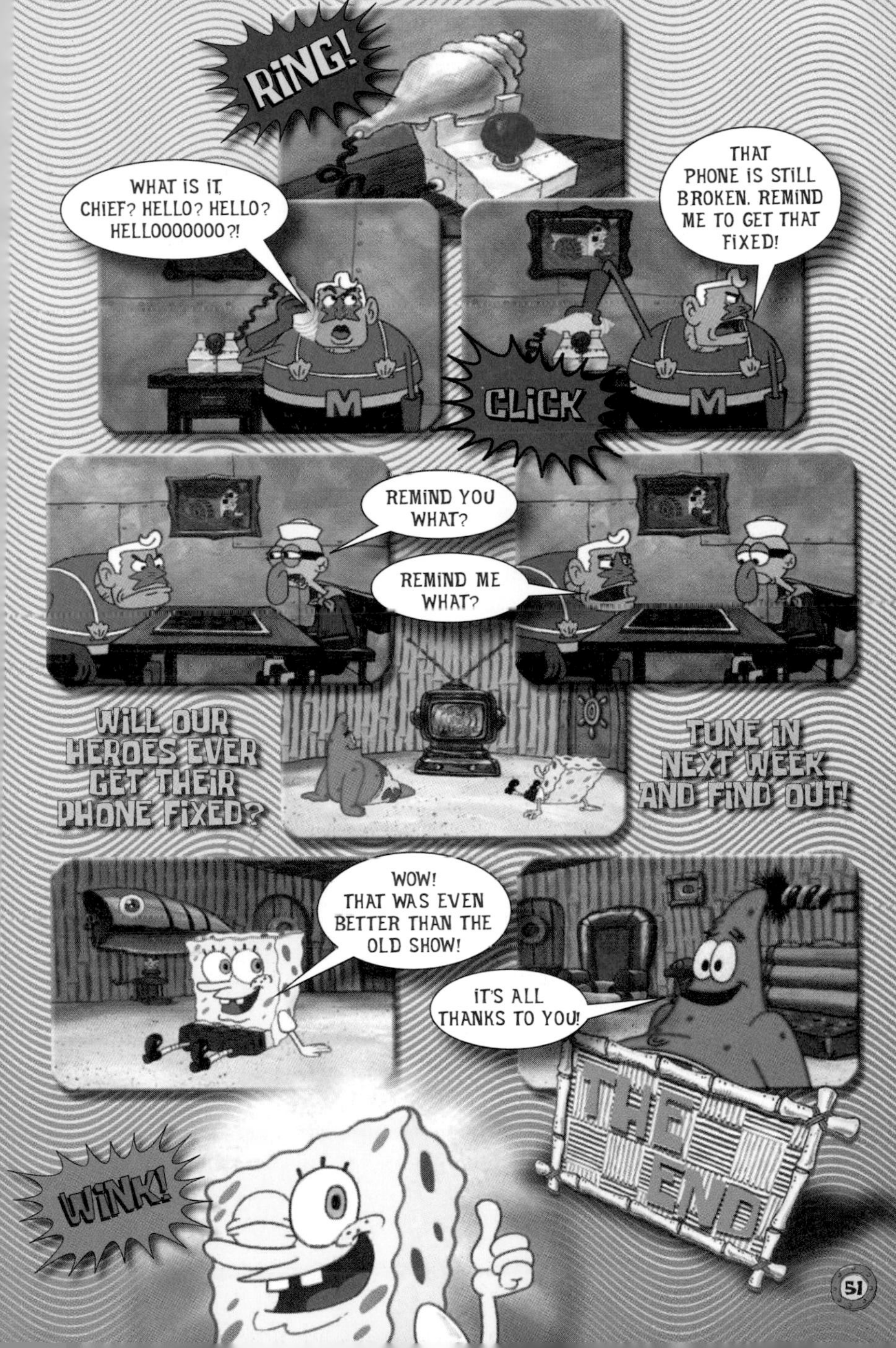
RING!
WHAT IS IT, CHIEF? HELLO? HELLO? HELLOOOOOOO?!
THAT PHONE IS STILL BROKEN. REMIND ME TO GET THAT FIXED!
CLICK
REMIND YOU WHAT?
REMIND ME WHAT?
WILL OUR HEROES EVER GET THEIR PHONE FIXED?
TUNE IN NEXT WEEK AND FIND OUT!
WOW! THAT WAS EVEN BETTER THAN THE OLD SHOW!
IT'S ALL THANKS TO YOU!
THE END
WINK!

SpongeBob SquarePants

Naughty Nautical Neighbors

by Jay Lender, Sam Henderson
and Mark O'Hare

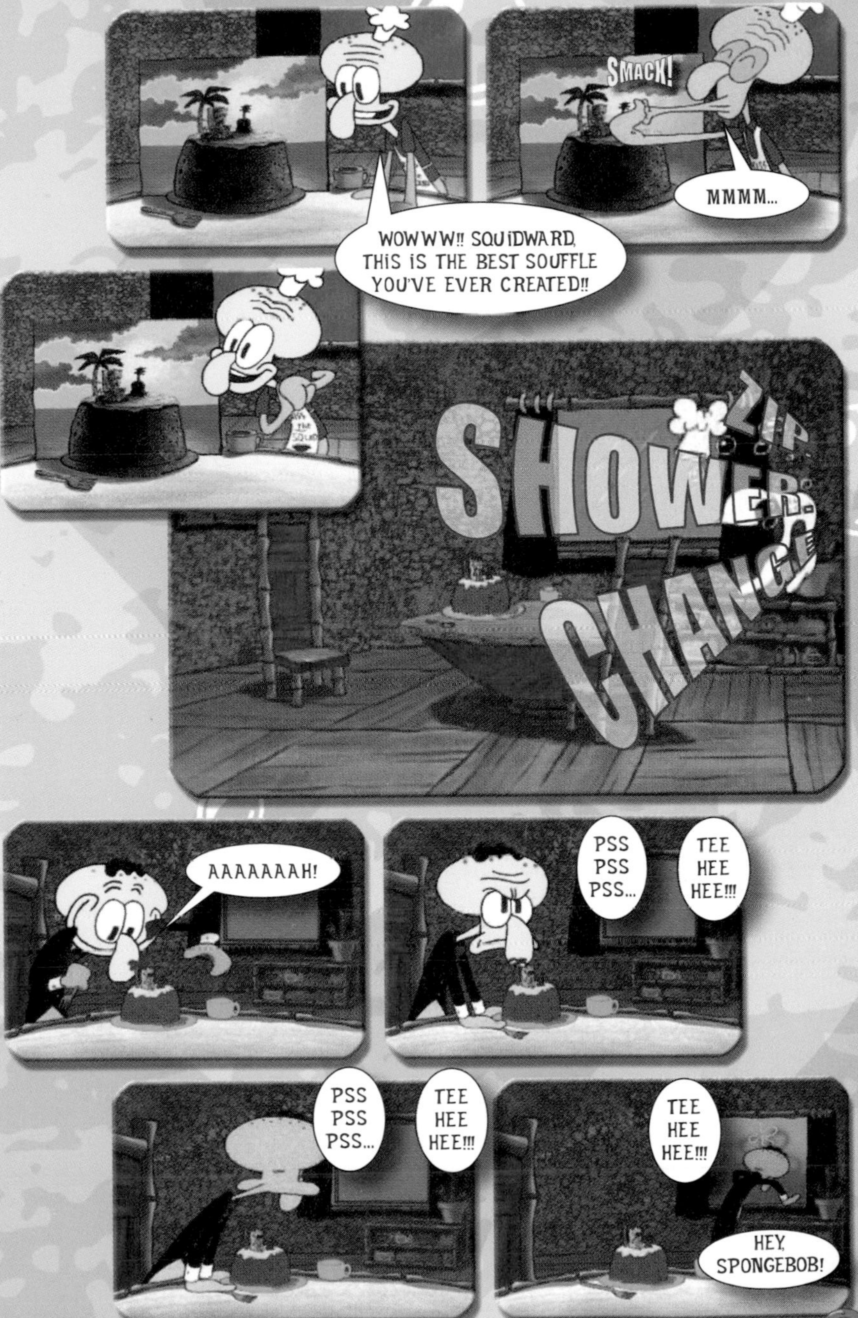

WOWWW!! SQUIDWARD, THIS IS THE BEST SOUFFLE YOU'VE EVER CREATED!!
SMACK!
MMMM...
SHOWER
ZIP
CHANGE
AAAAAAAH!
PSS PSS PSS...
TEE HEE HEE!!!
PSS PSS PSS...
TEE HEE HEE!!!
TEE HEE HEE!!!
HEY, SPONGEBOB!

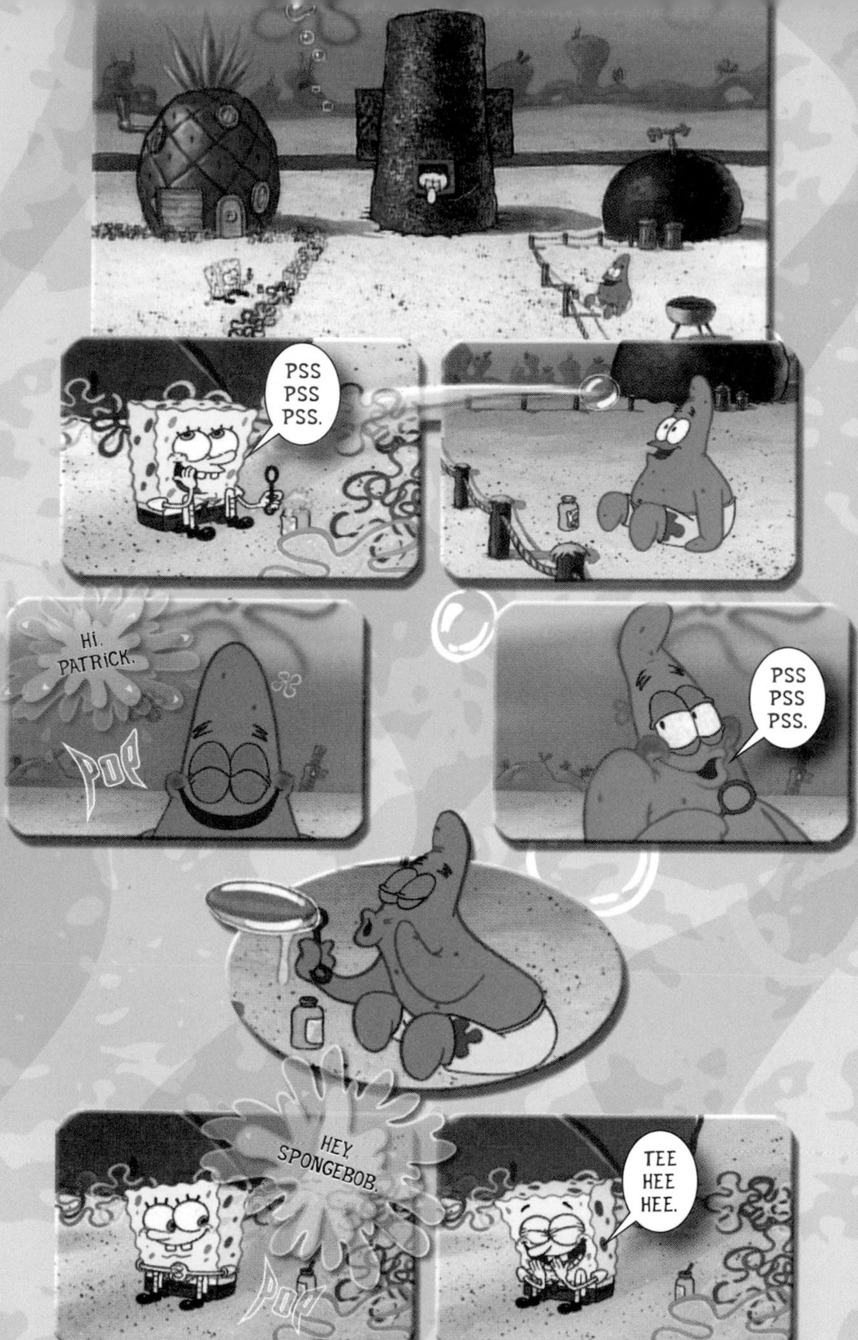
PSS
PSS
PSS.
HI,
PATRICK.
POP
PSS
PSS
PSS.
HEY,
SPONGEBOB.
POP
TEE
HEE
HEE.

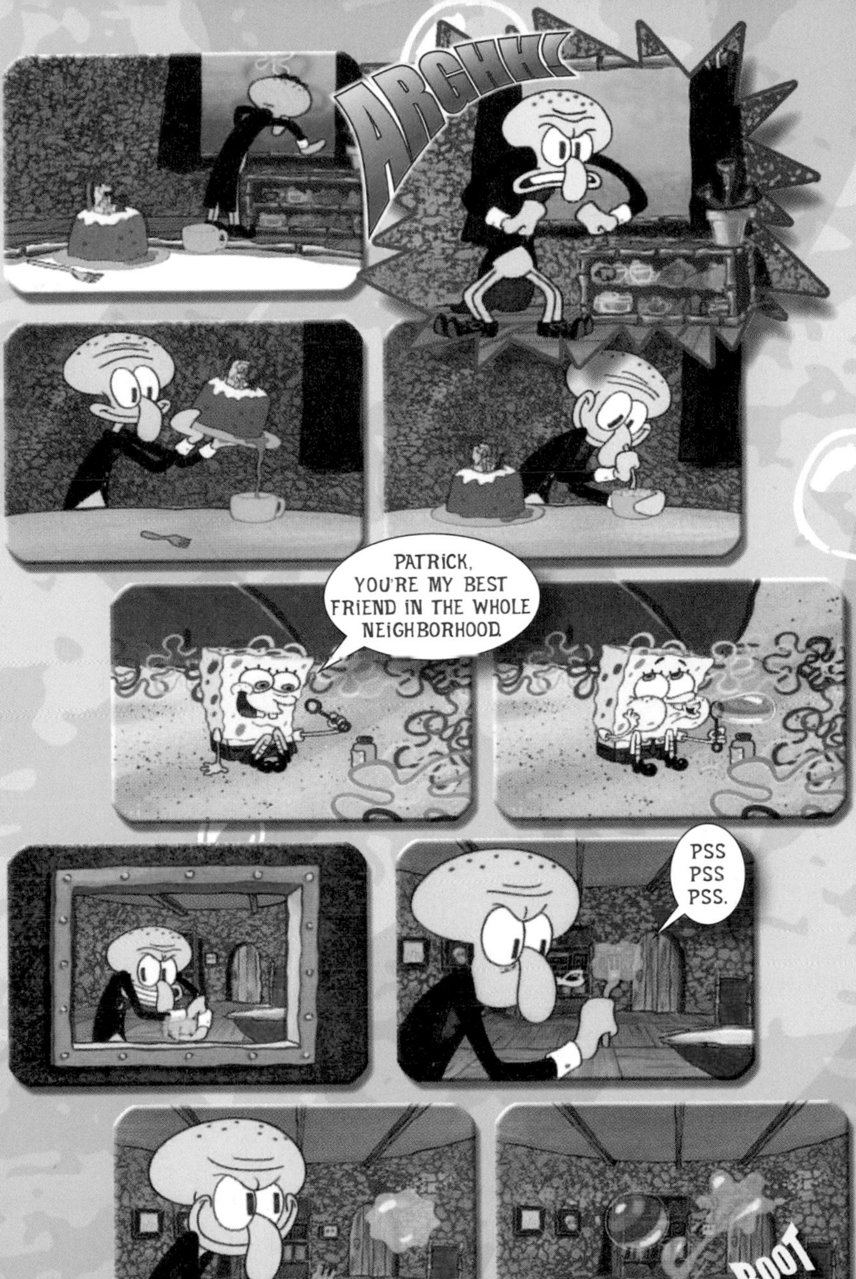
ARGHK!
PATRICK, YOU'RE MY BEST FRIEND IN THE WHOLE NEIGHBORHOOD.
PSS PSS PSS.
BOOT

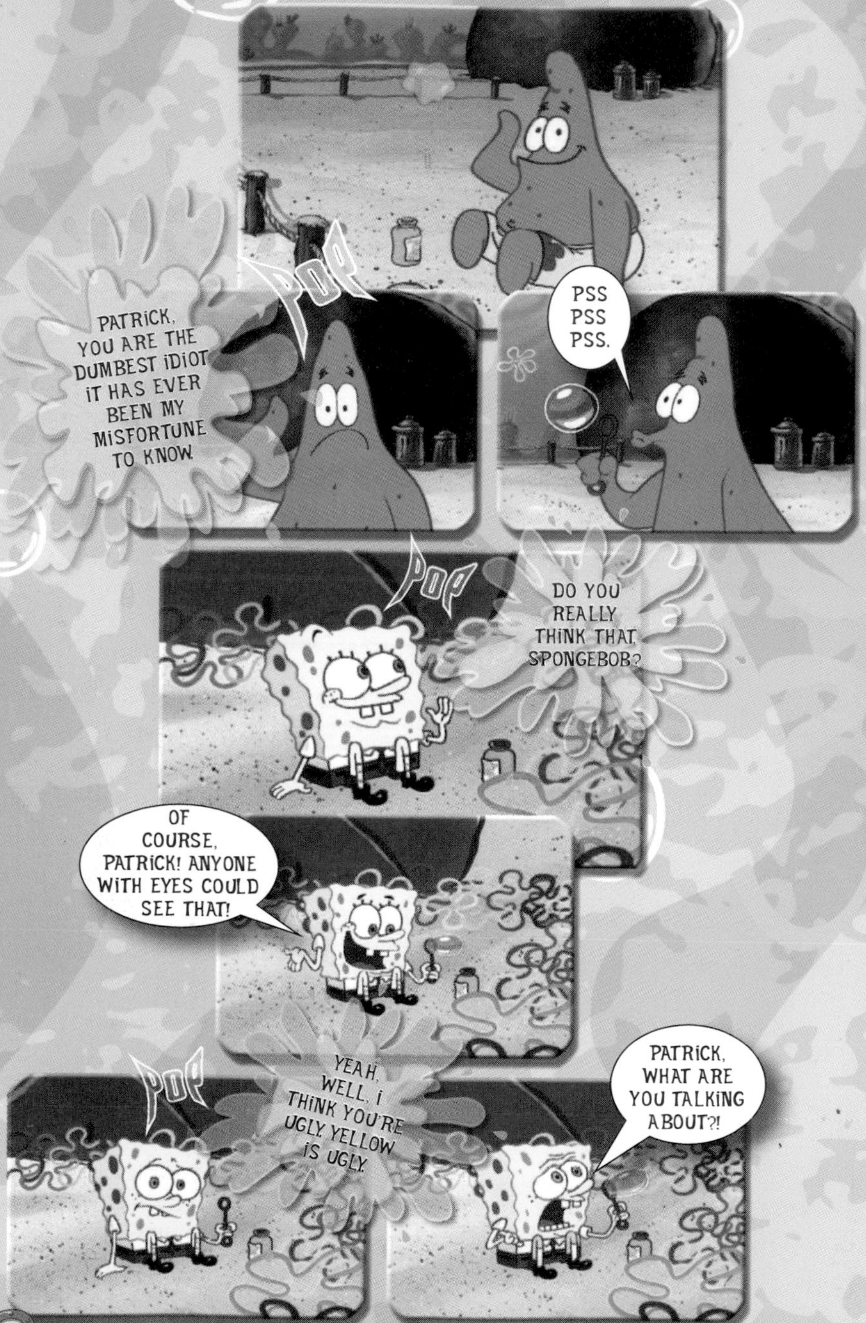
POP
PATRICK, YOU ARE THE DUMBEST IDIOT IT HAS EVER BEEN MY MISFORTUNE TO KNOW.
PSS PSS PSS.
POP
DO YOU REALLY THINK THAT, SPONGEBOB?
OF COURSE, PATRICK! ANYONE WITH EYES COULD SEE THAT!
POP
YEAH, WELL, I THINK YOU'RE UGLY. YELLOW IS UGLY.
PATRICK, WHAT ARE YOU TALKING ABOUT?!

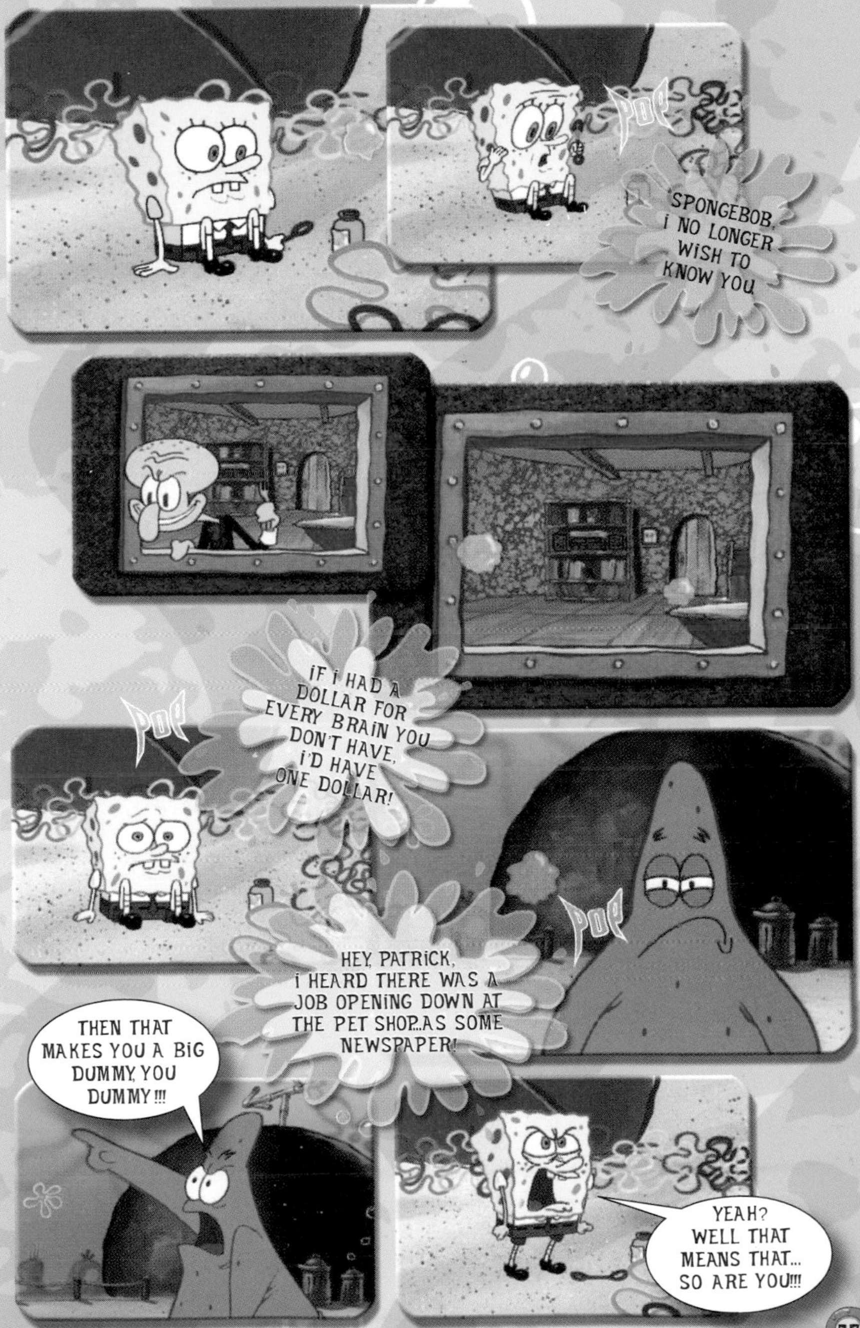
POP
SPONGEBOB, I NO LONGER WISH TO KNOW YOU.
IF I HAD A DOLLAR FOR EVERY BRAIN YOU DON'T HAVE, I'D HAVE ONE DOLLAR!
POP
POP
HEY, PATRICK, I HEARD THERE WAS A JOB OPENING DOWN AT THE PET SHOP...AS SOME NEWSPAPER!
THEN THAT MAKES YOU A BIG DUMMY, YOU DUMMY!!!
YEAH? WELL THAT MEANS THAT... SO ARE YOU!!!

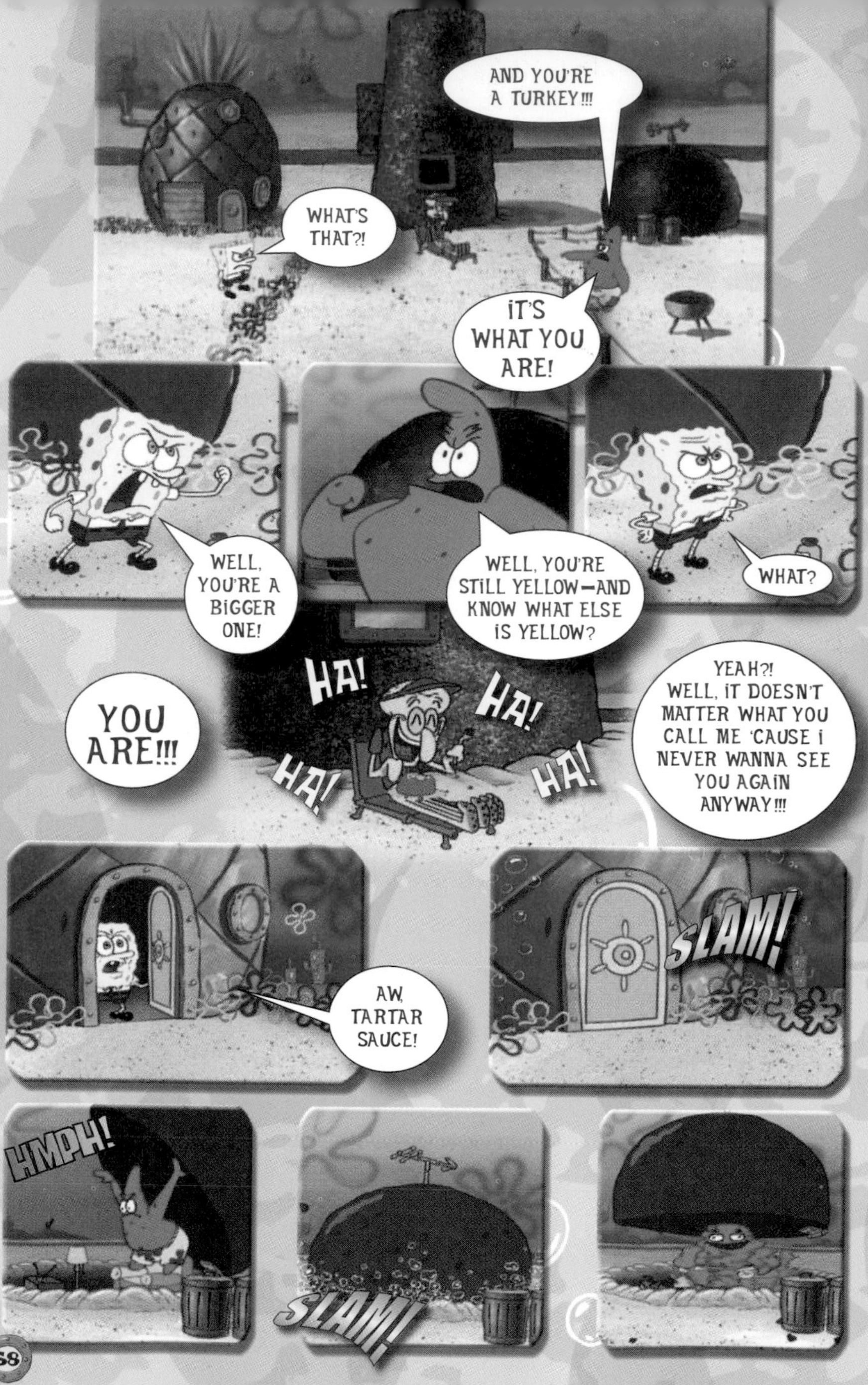
AND YOU'RE A TURKEY!!!
WHAT'S THAT?!
IT'S WHAT YOU ARE!
WELL, YOU'RE A BIGGER ONE!
WELL, YOU'RE STILL YELLOW—AND KNOW WHAT ELSE IS YELLOW?
WHAT?
YOU ARE!!!
HA!
HA!
HA!
HA!
YEAH?! WELL, IT DOESN'T MATTER WHAT YOU CALL ME 'CAUSE I NEVER WANNA SEE YOU AGAIN ANYWAY!!!
AW, TARTAR SAUCE!
SLAM!
HMPH!
SLAM!

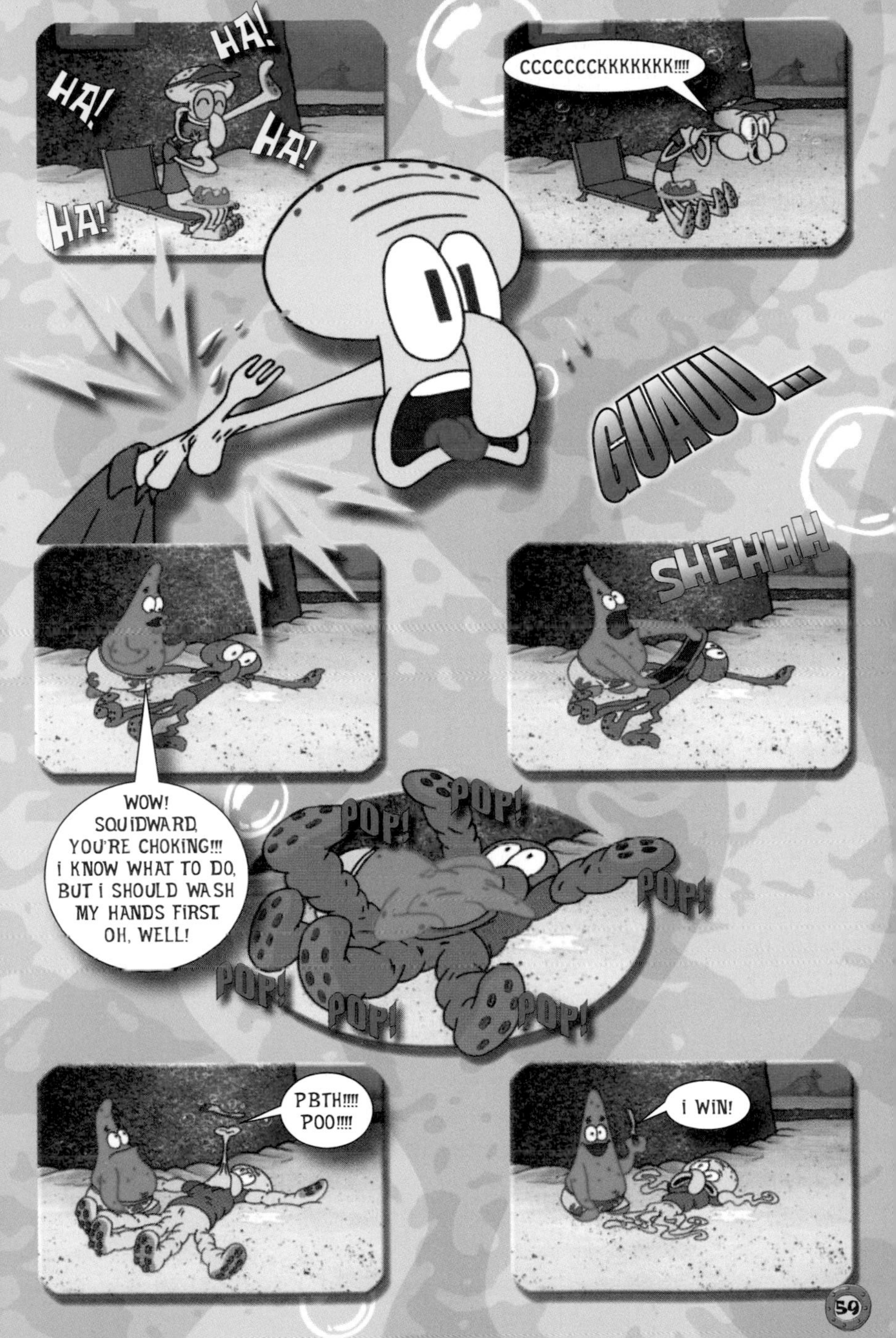
HA!
HA!
HA!
HA!
CCCCCCCKKKKKKK!!!!
GUAUU...
SHEHHH
WOW! SQUIDWARD, YOU'RE CHOKING!!! I KNOW WHAT TO DO, BUT I SHOULD WASH MY HANDS FIRST. OH, WELL!
POP!
POP!
POP!
POP!
POP!
POP!
PBTH!!!! POO!!!!
I WIN!

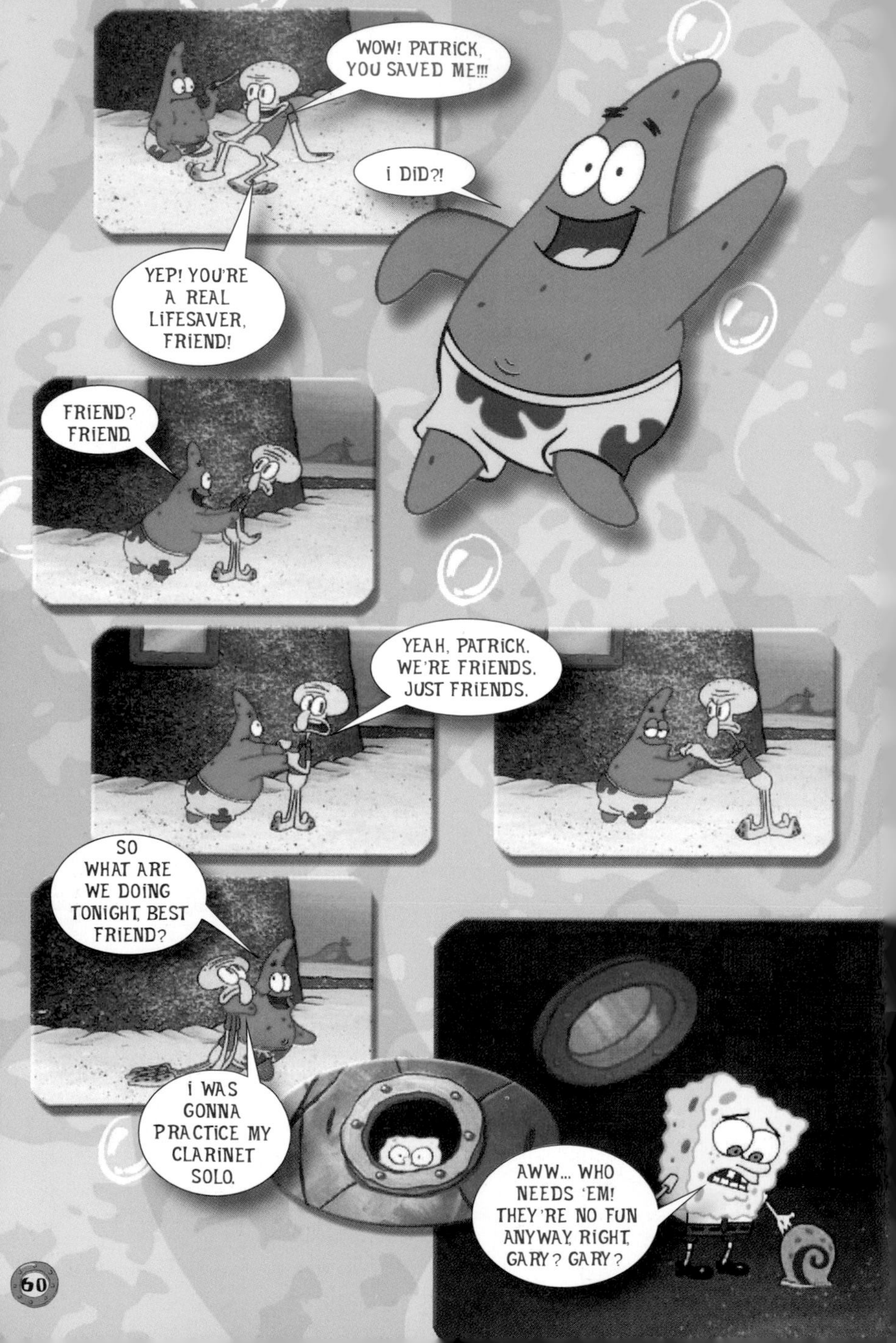

WOW! PATRICK, YOU SAVED ME!!!
I DID?!
YEP! YOU'RE A REAL LIFESAVER, FRIEND!
FRIEND? FRIEND.
YEAH, PATRICK. WE'RE FRIENDS. JUST FRIENDS.
SO WHAT ARE WE DOING TONIGHT, BEST FRIEND?
I WAS GONNA PRACTICE MY CLARINET SOLO.
AWW... WHO NEEDS 'EM! THEY'RE NO FUN ANYWAY, RIGHT, GARY? GARY?

TONIGHT, SQUIDWARD WILL BE PERFORMING HIS VERSION OF "SOLITUDE IN E MINOR".

CLAP CLAP CLAP

E-MINOR, ALL RIGHT! YEAH, YEAH!!

SNOOOOOOOORE...

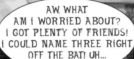

AW, WHAT AM I WORRIED ABOUT? I GOT PLENTY OF FRIENDS! I COULD NAME THREE RIGHT OFF THE BAT! UH...

SCRIBBLE. SCRIBBLE.

THE GANG'S ALL HERE.

SNIFF

SNIFF

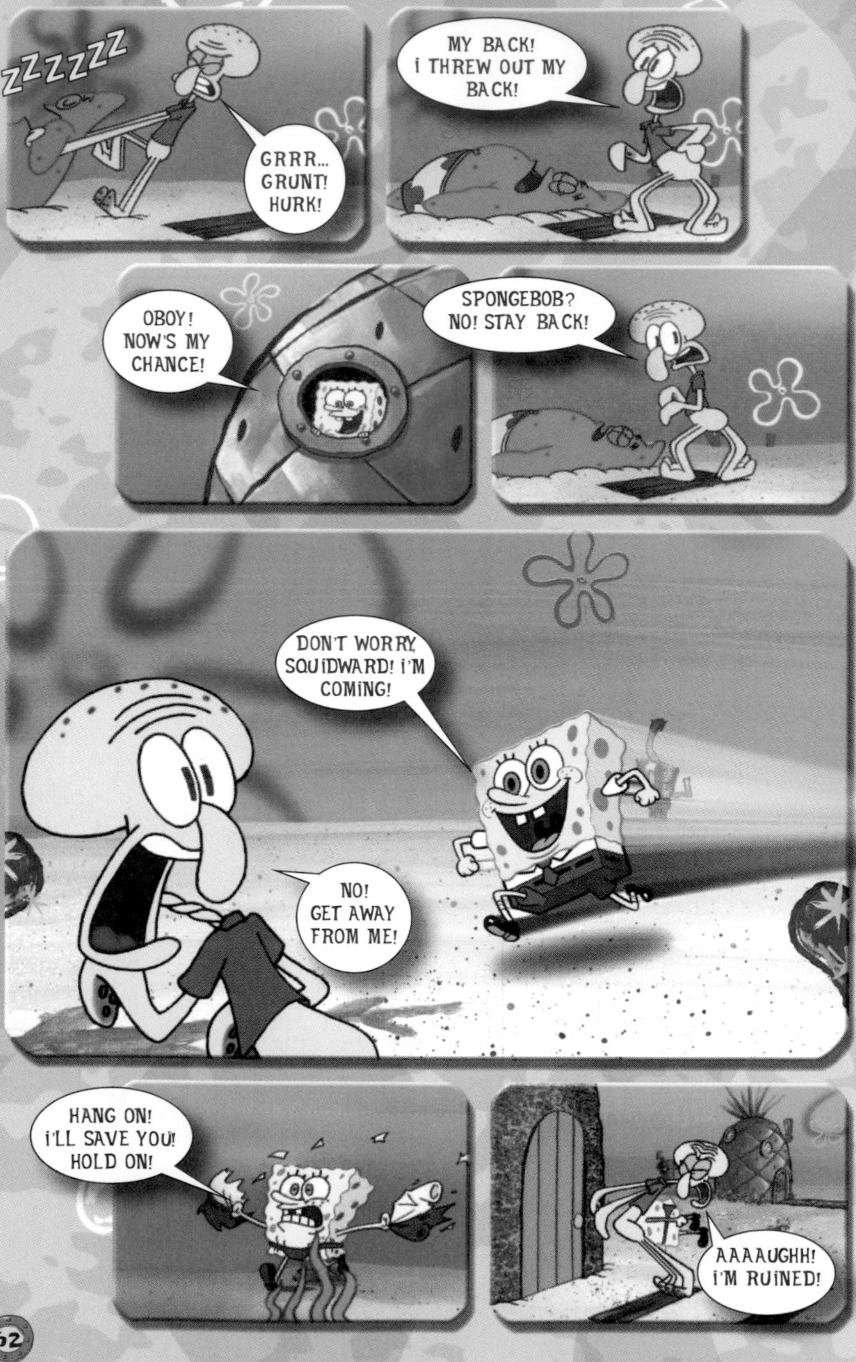
ZZZZZZ
GRRR... GRUNT! HURK!
MY BACK! I THREW OUT MY BACK!
OBOY! NOW'S MY CHANCE!
SPONGEBOB? NO! STAY BACK!
DON'T WORRY, SQUIDWARD! I'M COMING!
NO! GET AWAY FROM ME!
HANG ON! I'LL SAVE YOU! HOLD ON!
AAAAUGHH! I'M RUINED!

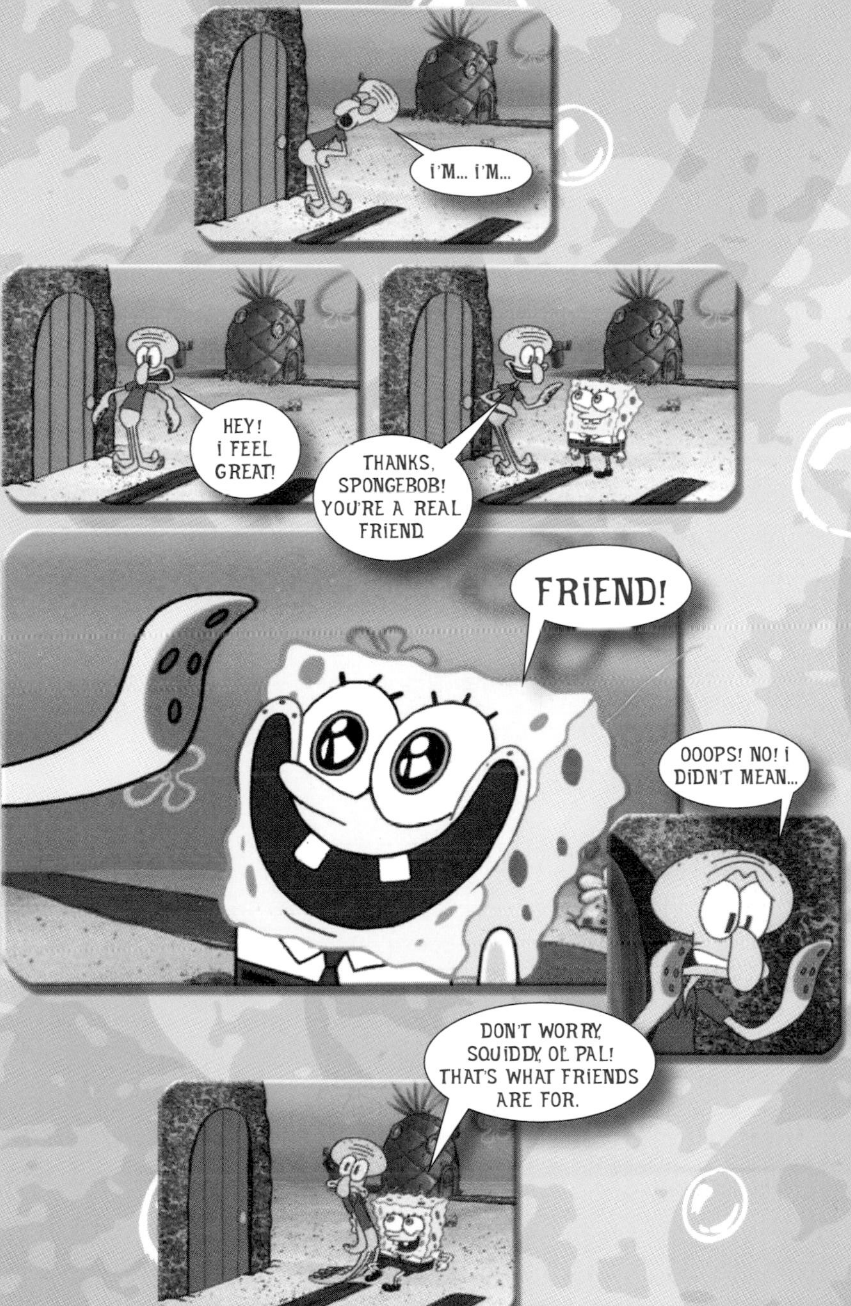
I'M... I'M...
HEY! I FEEL GREAT!
THANKS, SPONGEBOB! YOU'RE A REAL FRIEND.
FRIEND!
OOOPS! NO! I DIDN'T MEAN...
DON'T WORRY, SQUIDDY, OL' PAL! THAT'S WHAT FRIENDS ARE FOR.

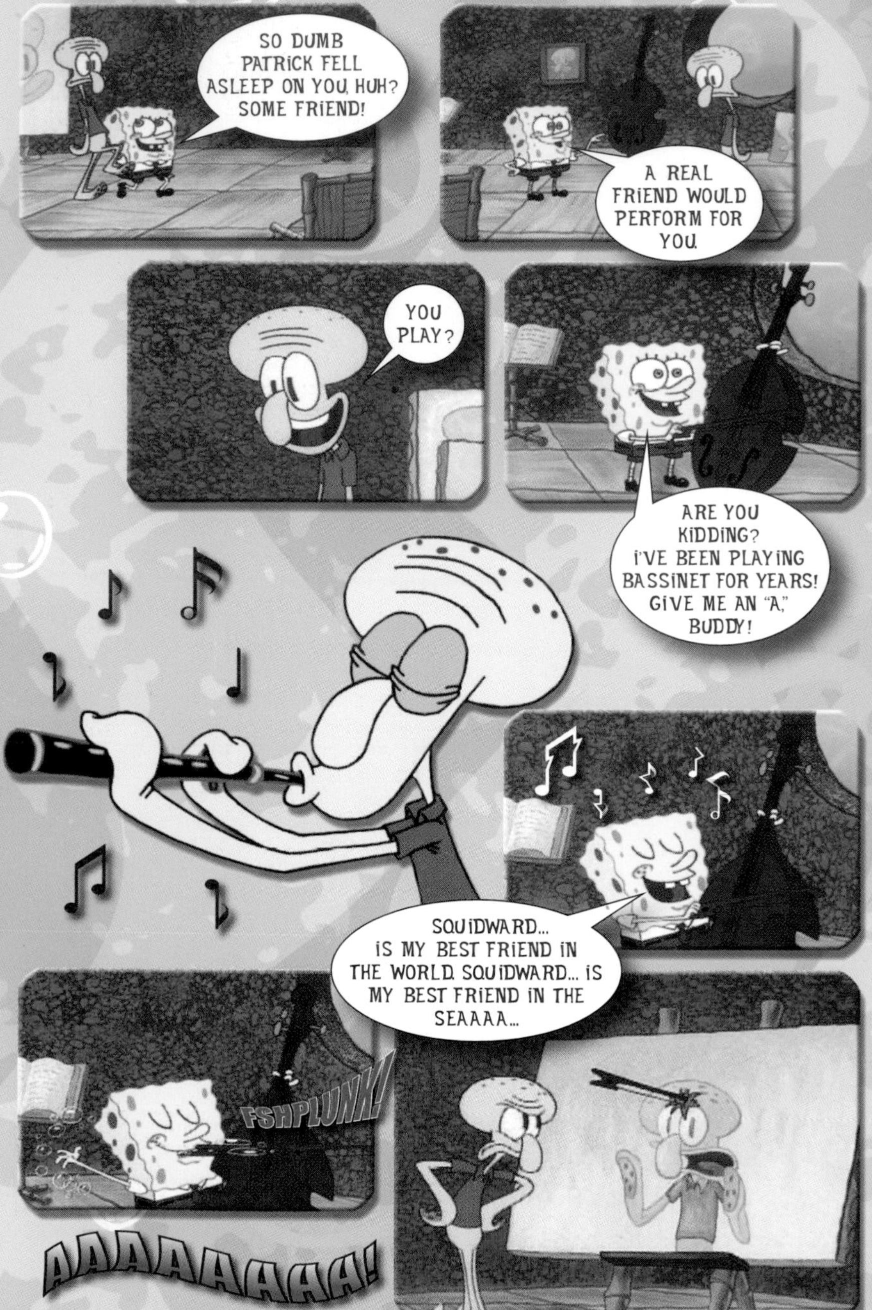
SO DUMB PATRICK FELL ASLEEP ON YOU, HUH? SOME FRIEND!
A REAL FRIEND WOULD PERFORM FOR YOU.
YOU PLAY?
ARE YOU KIDDING? I'VE BEEN PLAYING BASSINET FOR YEARS! GIVE ME AN "A," BUDDY!
SQUIDWARD... IS MY BEST FRIEND IN THE WORLD. SQUIDWARD... IS MY BEST FRIEND IN THE SEAAAA...
FSHPLUNK!
AAAAAAAA!

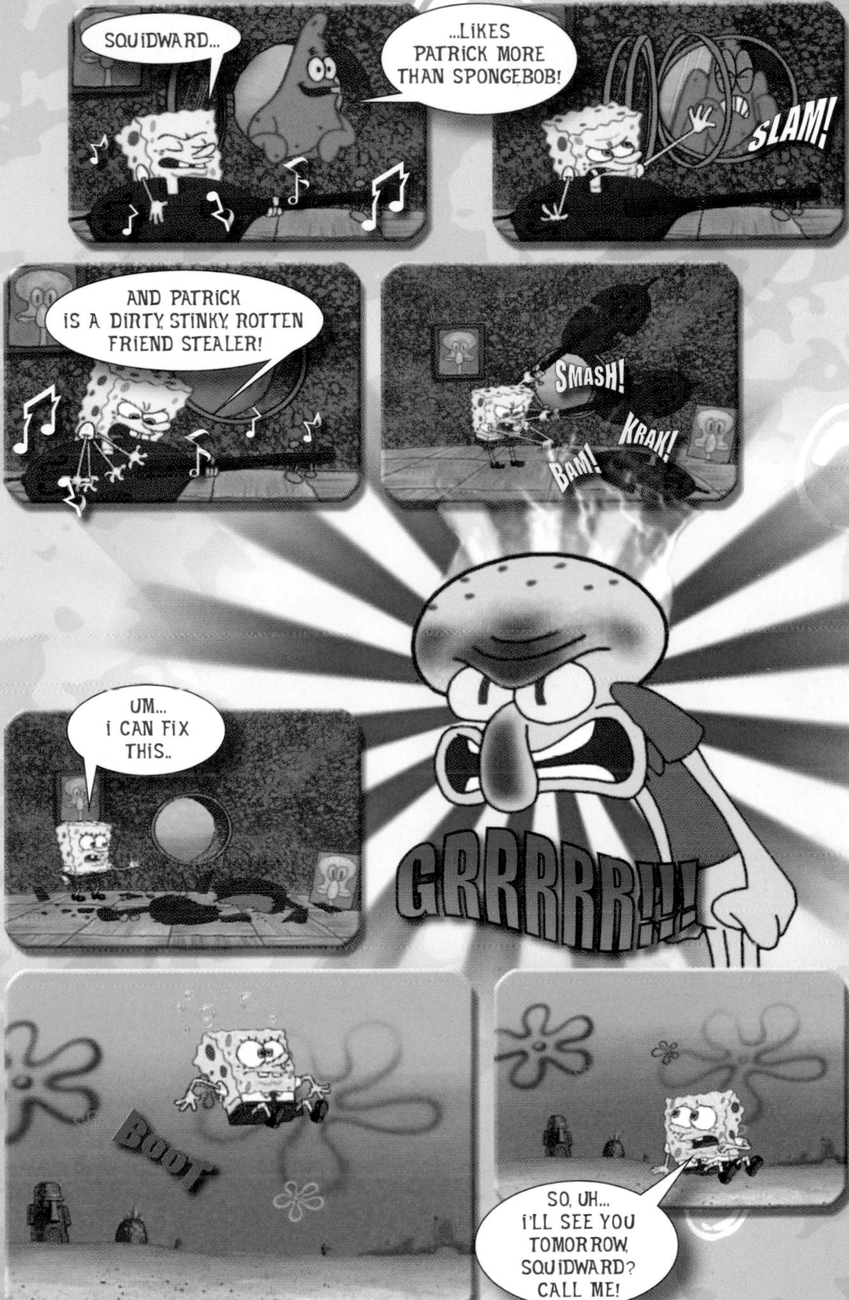
SQUIDWARD...
...LIKES PATRICK MORE THAN SPONGEBOB!
SLAM!
AND PATRICK IS A DIRTY, STINKY, ROTTEN FRIEND STEALER!
SMASH!
KRAK!
BAM!
UM... I CAN FIX THIS..
GRRRRR!!!
BOOT
SO, UH... I'LL SEE YOU TOMORROW, SQUIDWARD? CALL ME!

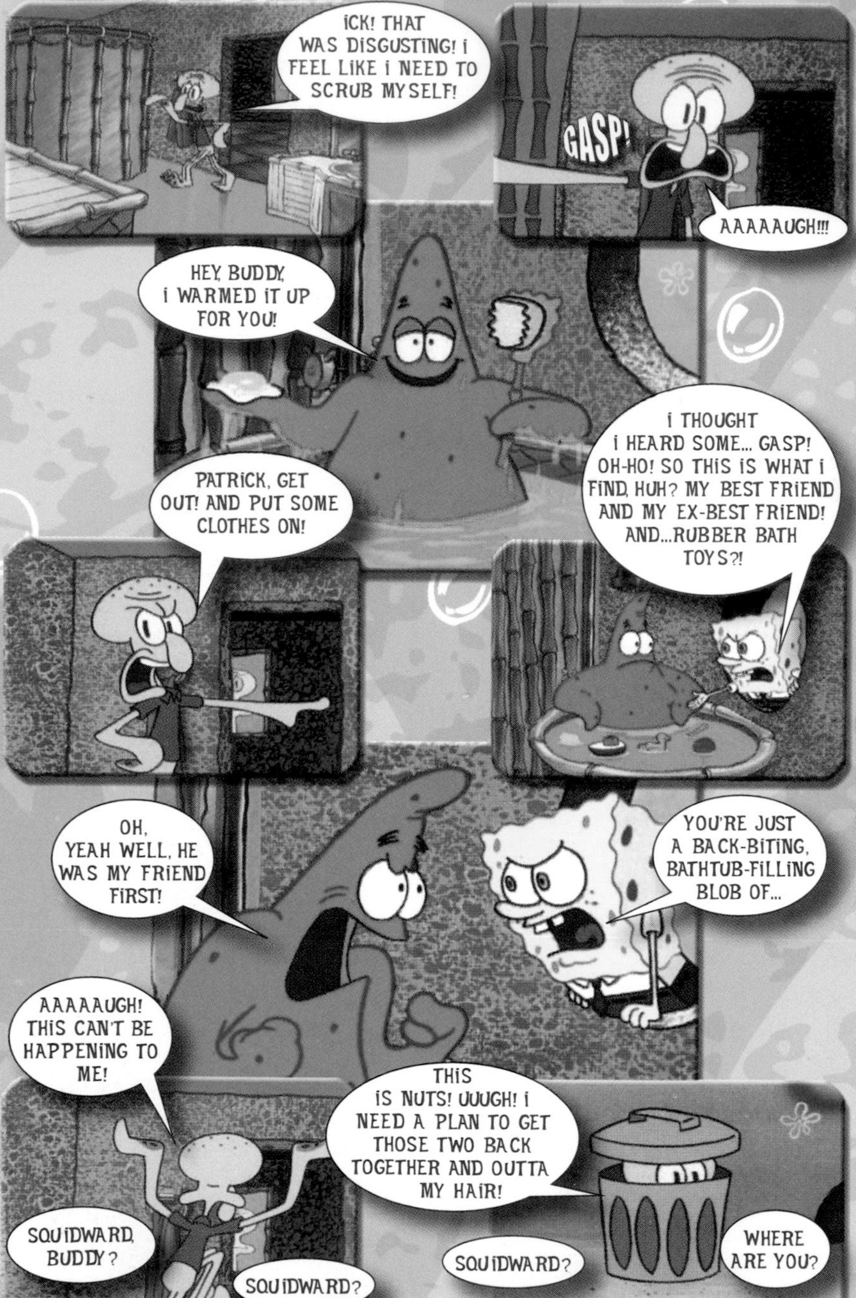
ICK! THAT WAS DISGUSTING! I FEEL LIKE I NEED TO SCRUB MYSELF!
GASP!
AAAAAUGH!!!
HEY, BUDDY, I WARMED IT UP FOR YOU!
PATRICK, GET OUT! AND PUT SOME CLOTHES ON!
I THOUGHT I HEARD SOME... GASP! OH-HO! SO THIS IS WHAT I FIND, HUH? MY BEST FRIEND AND MY EX-BEST FRIEND! AND...RUBBER BATH TOYS?!
OH, YEAH WELL, HE WAS MY FRIEND FIRST!
YOU'RE JUST A BACK-BITING, BATHTUB-FILLING BLOB OF...
AAAAAUGH! THIS CAN'T BE HAPPENING TO ME!
SQUIDWARD, BUDDY?
SQUIDWARD?
THIS IS NUTS! UUUGH! I NEED A PLAN TO GET THOSE TWO BACK TOGETHER AND OUTTA MY HAIR!
SQUIDWARD?
WHERE ARE YOU?

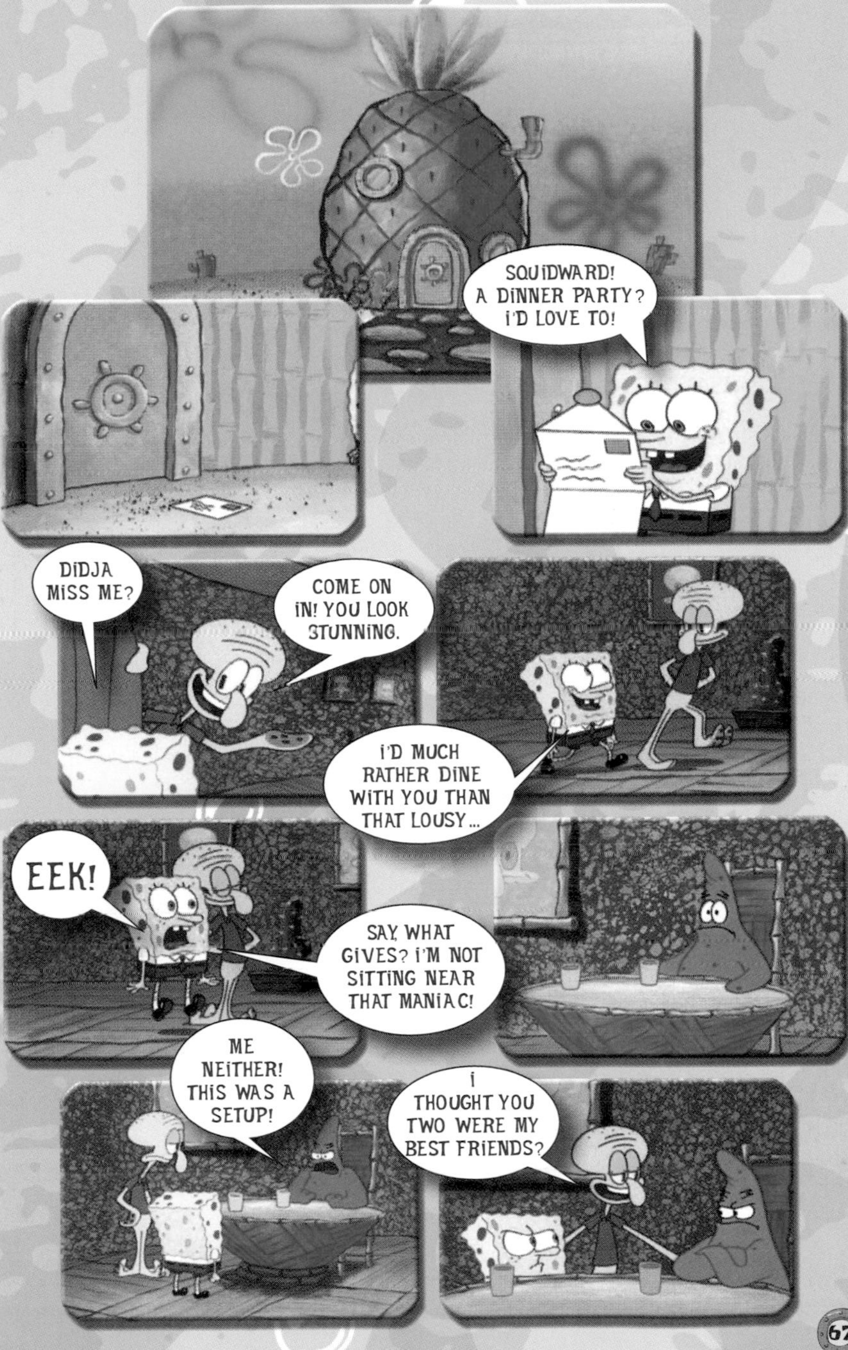
SQUIDWARD! A DINNER PARTY? I'D LOVE TO!
DIDJA MISS ME?
COME ON IN! YOU LOOK STUNNING.
I'D MUCH RATHER DINE WITH YOU THAN THAT LOUSY...
EEK!
SAY, WHAT GIVES? I'M NOT SITTING NEAR THAT MANIAC!
ME NEITHER! THIS WAS A SETUP!
I THOUGHT YOU TWO WERE MY BEST FRIENDS?

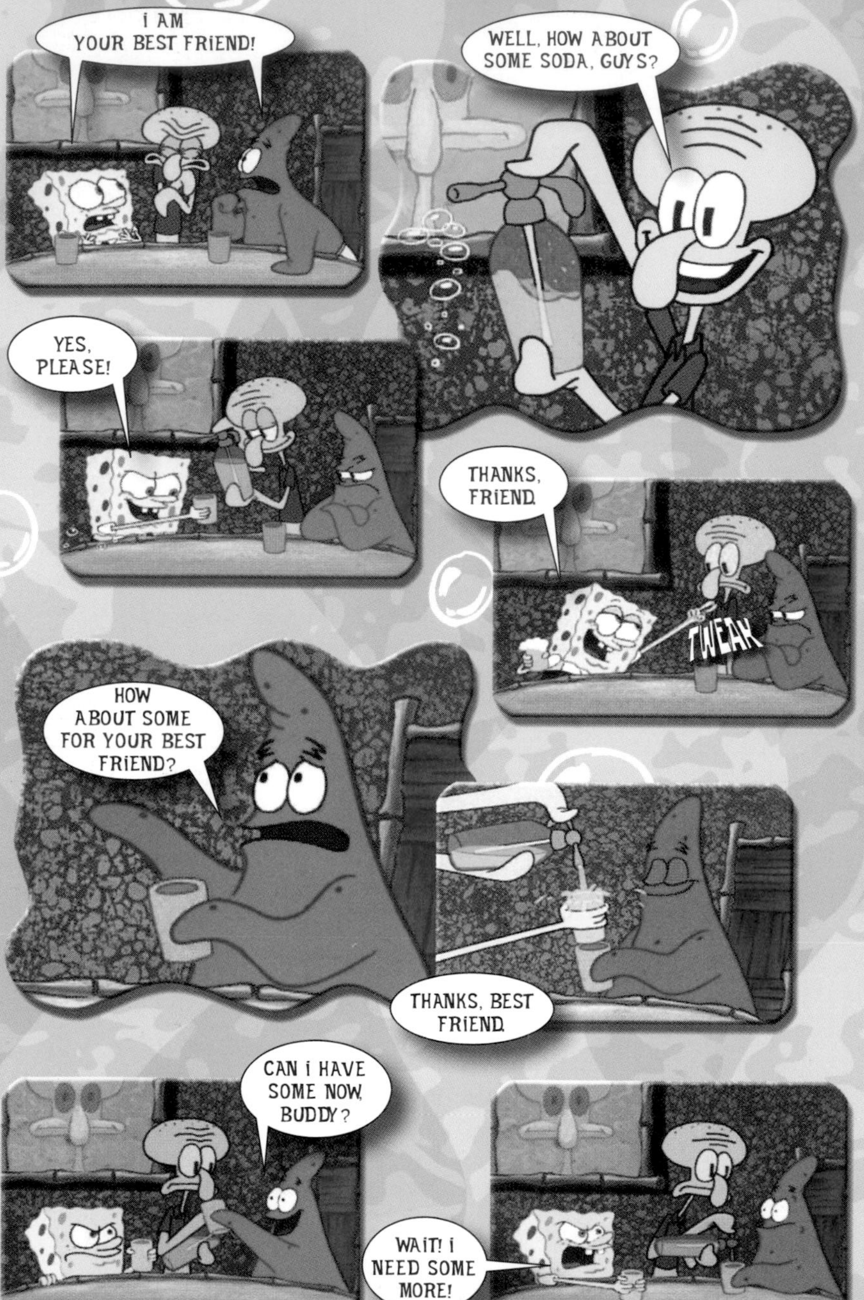
I AM YOUR BEST FRIEND!
WELL, HOW ABOUT SOME SODA, GUYS?
YES, PLEASE!
THANKS, FRIEND.
TWEAK
HOW ABOUT SOME FOR YOUR BEST FRIEND?
THANKS, BEST FRIEND.
CAN I HAVE SOME NOW, BUDDY?
WAIT! I NEED SOME MORE!

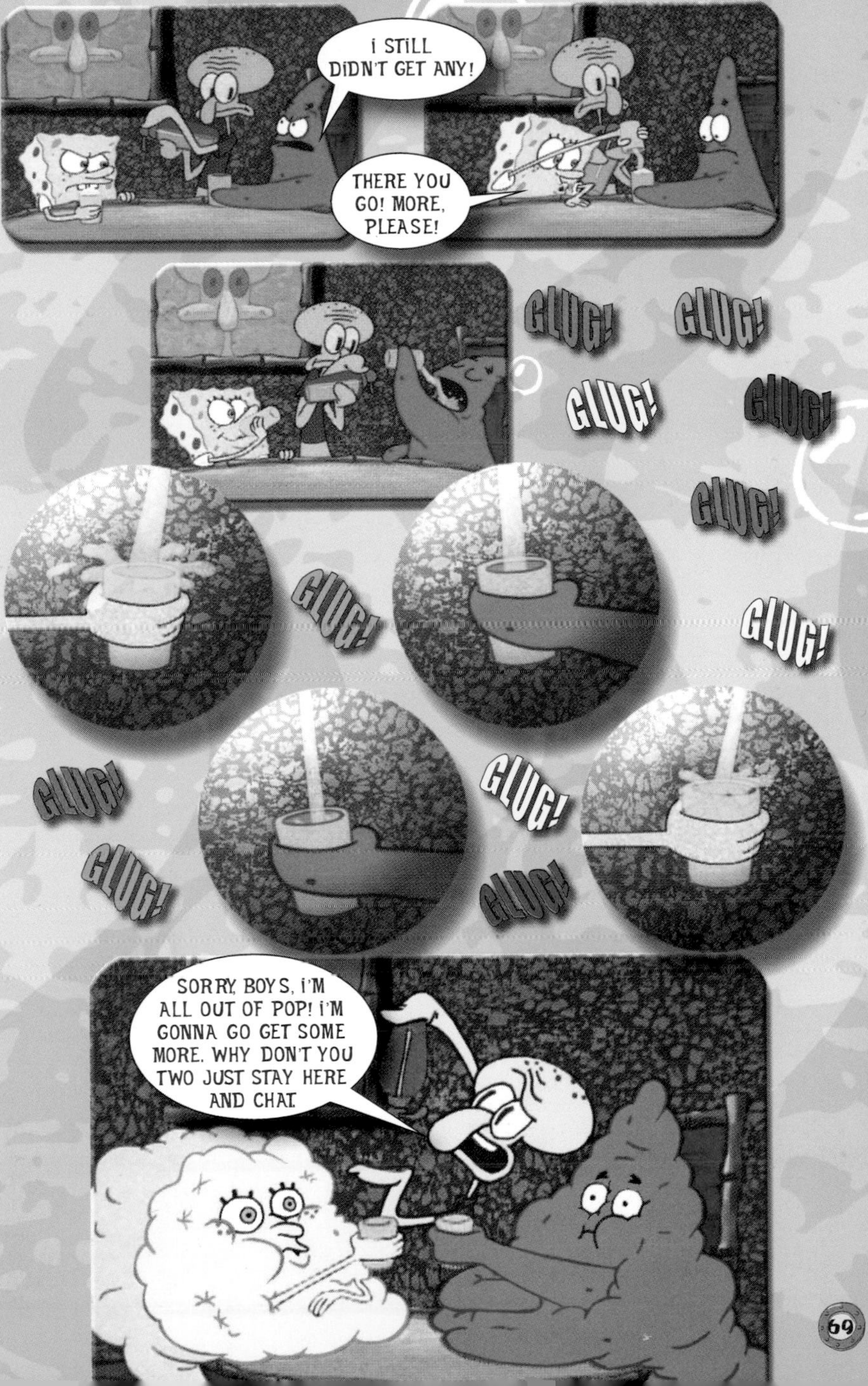
I STILL DIDN'T GET ANY!
THERE YOU GO! MORE, PLEASE!
GLUG!
GLUG!
GLUG!
GLUG!
GLUG!
GLUG!
GLUG!
GLUG!
GLUG!
GLUG!
GLUG!
SORRY, BOYS, I'M ALL OUT OF POP! I'M GONNA GO GET SOME MORE. WHY DON'T YOU TWO JUST STAY HERE AND CHAT.

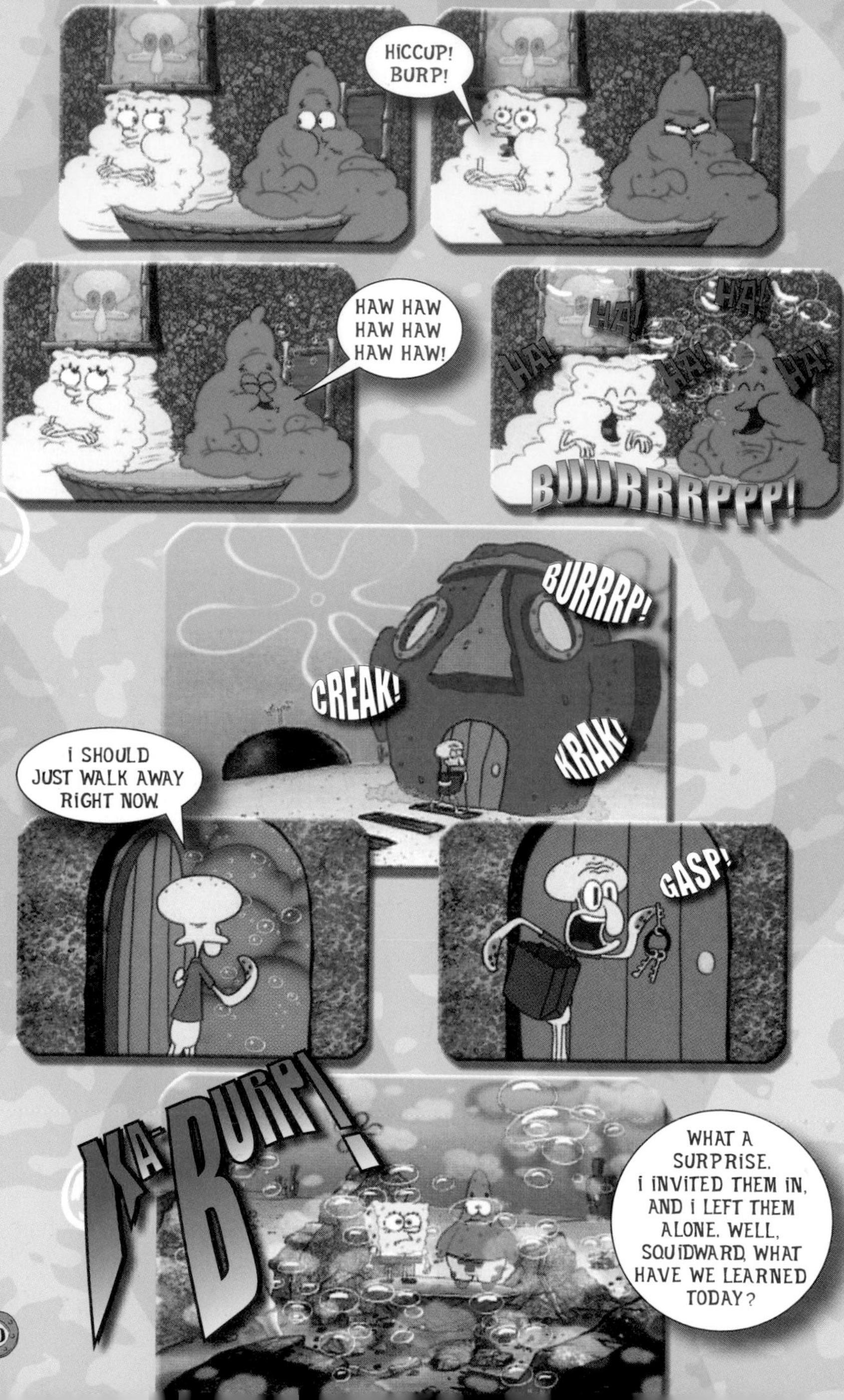
HICCUP! BURP!
HAW HAW HAW HAW HAW HAW!
HA! HA! HA! HA! HA!
BUURRRPPP!
BURRRP!
CREAK!
KRAK!
I SHOULD JUST WALK AWAY RIGHT NOW.
GASP!
KA-BURP!
WHAT A SURPRISE. I INVITED THEM IN, AND I LEFT THEM ALONE. WELL, SQUIDWARD, WHAT HAVE WE LEARNED TODAY?

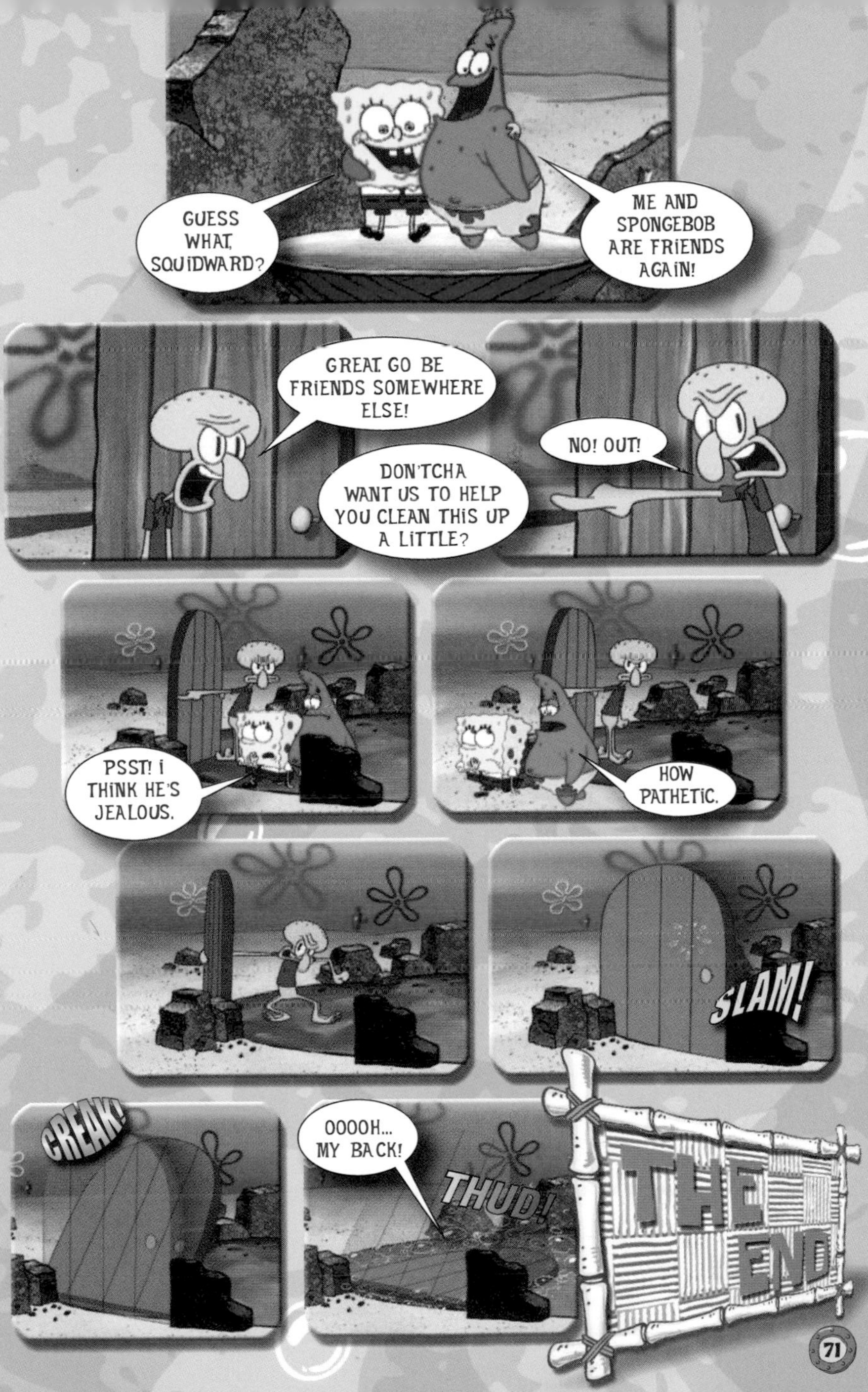
GUESS WHAT, SQUIDWARD?
ME AND SPONGEBOB ARE FRIENDS AGAIN!
GREAT. GO BE FRIENDS SOMEWHERE ELSE!
DON'TCHA WANT US TO HELP YOU CLEAN THIS UP A LITTLE?
NO! OUT!
PSST! I THINK HE'S JEALOUS.
HOW PATHETIC.
SLAM!
CREAK!
OOOOH... MY BACK!
THUD!
THE END

SPONGEBOB SQUAREPANTS™

Wet Painters

by Jay Lender, Sam Henderson
and Mark O'Hare

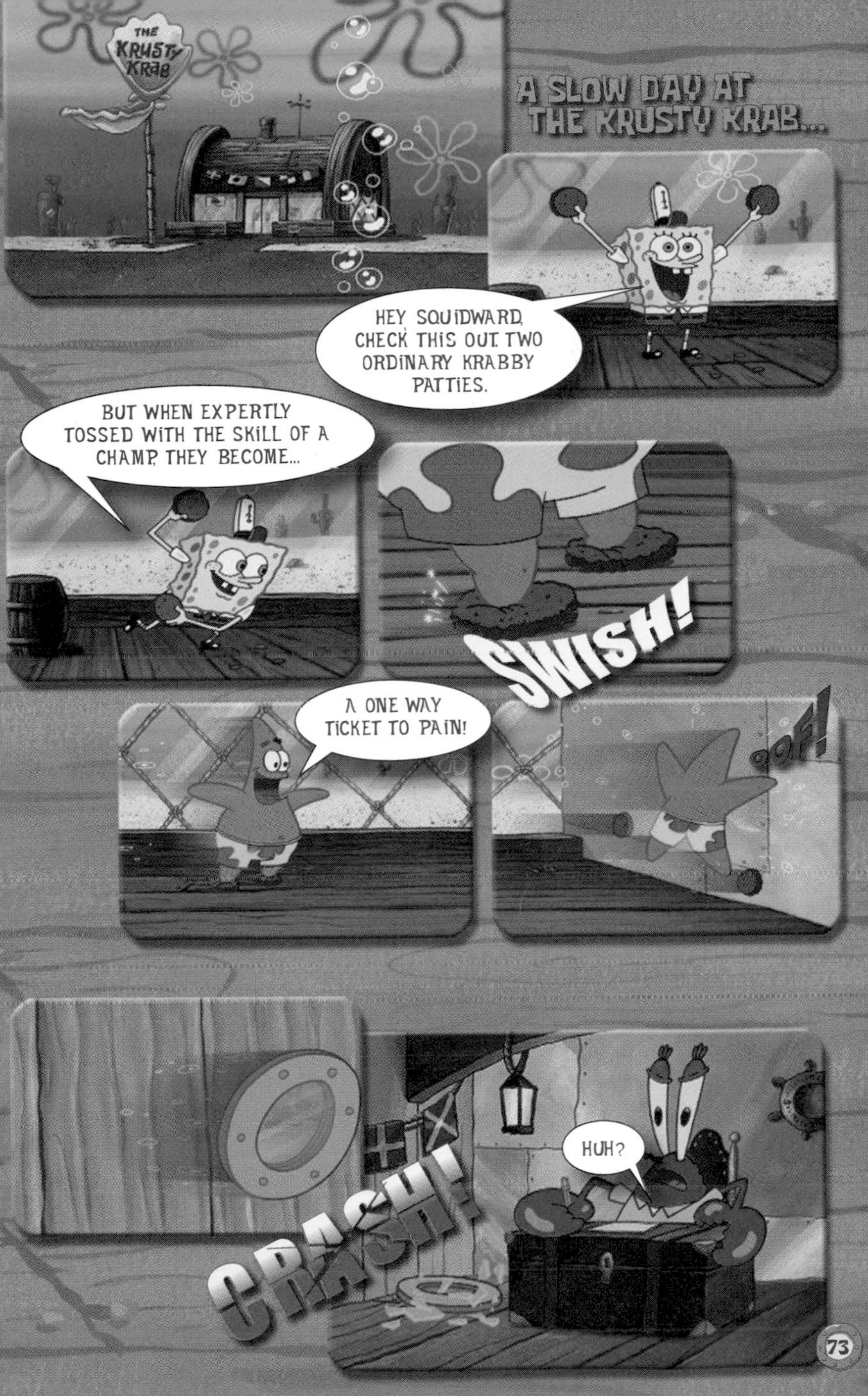
THE KRUSTY KRAB
A SLOW DAY AT THE KRUSTY KRAB...
HEY SQUIDWARD, CHECK THIS OUT. TWO ORDINARY KRABBY PATTIES.
BUT WHEN EXPERTLY TOSSED WITH THE SKILL OF A CHAMP, THEY BECOME...
SWISH!
A ONE WAY TICKET TO PAIN!
OOF!
CRASH!
CRASH!
HUH?

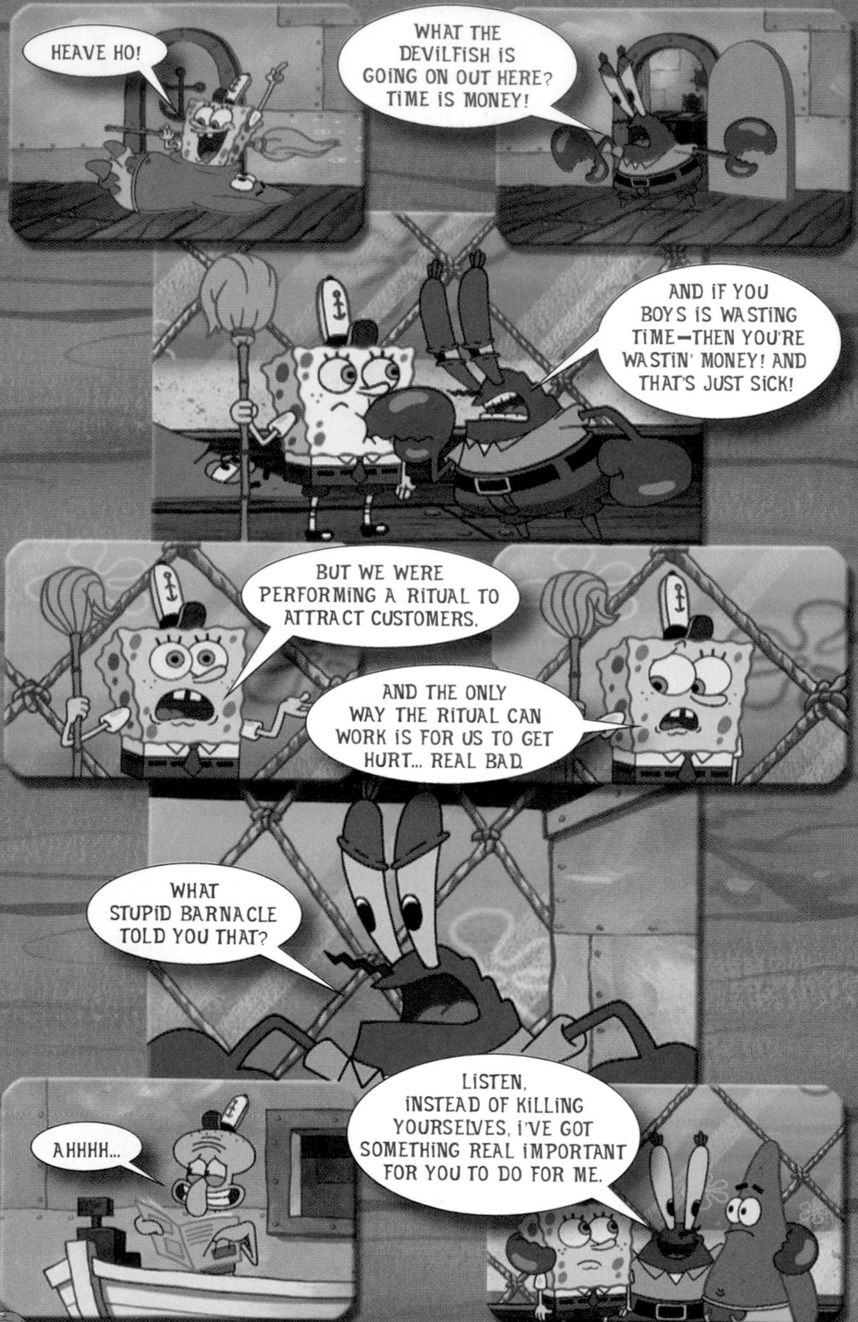
HEAVE HO!
WHAT THE DEVILFISH IS GOING ON OUT HERE? TIME IS MONEY!
AND IF YOU BOYS IS WASTING TIME—THEN YOU'RE WASTIN' MONEY! AND THAT'S JUST SICK!
BUT WE WERE PERFORMING A RITUAL TO ATTRACT CUSTOMERS.
AND THE ONLY WAY THE RITUAL CAN WORK IS FOR US TO GET HURT... REAL BAD.
WHAT STUPID BARNACLE TOLD YOU THAT?
AHHHH...
LISTEN, INSTEAD OF KILLING YOURSELVES, I'VE GOT SOMETHING REAL IMPORTANT FOR YOU TO DO FOR ME.

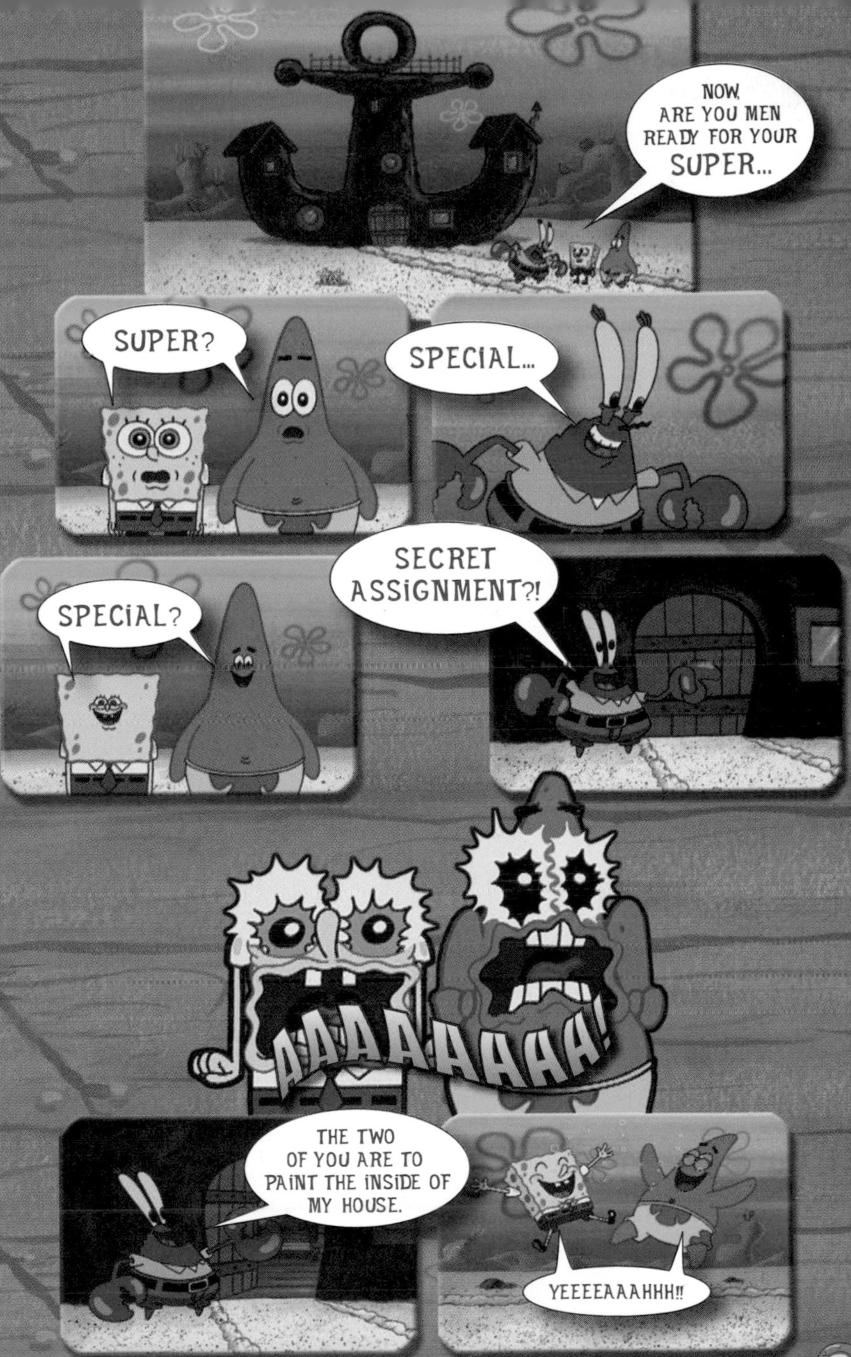
NOW, ARE YOU MEN READY FOR YOUR SUPER...
SUPER?
SPECIAL...
SPECIAL?
SECRET ASSIGNMENT?!
AAAAAAAA!
THE TWO OF YOU ARE TO PAINT THE INSIDE OF MY HOUSE.
YEEEEAAAHHH!!

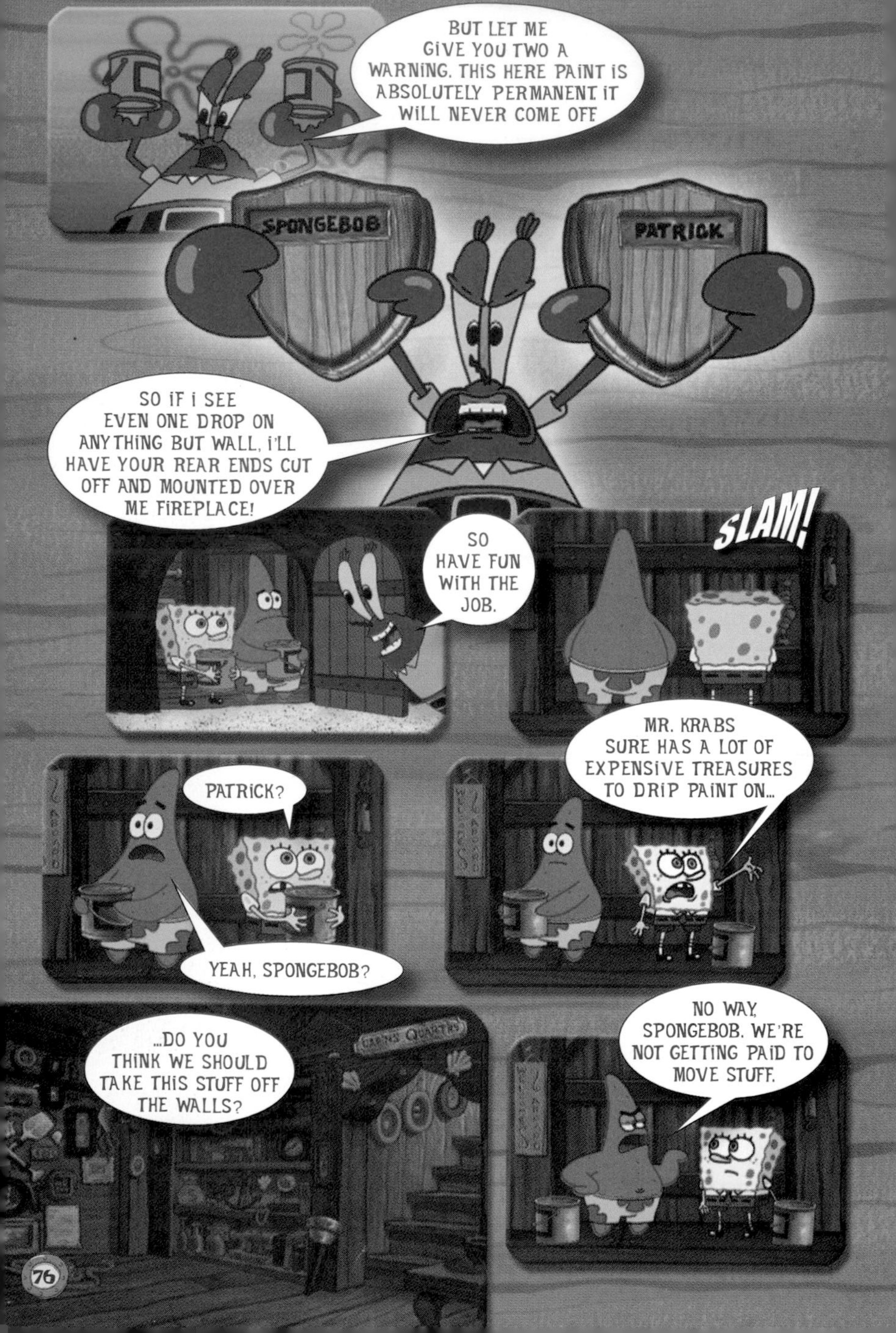
BUT LET ME GIVE YOU TWO A WARNING. THIS HERE PAINT IS ABSOLUTELY PERMANENT. IT WILL NEVER COME OFF.
SPONGEBOB
PATRICK
SO IF I SEE EVEN ONE DROP ON ANYTHING BUT WALL, I'LL HAVE YOUR REAR ENDS CUT OFF AND MOUNTED OVER ME FIREPLACE!
SO HAVE FUN WITH THE JOB.
SLAM!
PATRICK?
YEAH, SPONGEBOB?
MR. KRABS SURE HAS A LOT OF EXPENSIVE TREASURES TO DRIP PAINT ON...
...DO YOU THINK WE SHOULD TAKE THIS STUFF OFF THE WALLS?
NO WAY, SPONGEBOB. WE'RE NOT GETTING PAID TO MOVE STUFF.

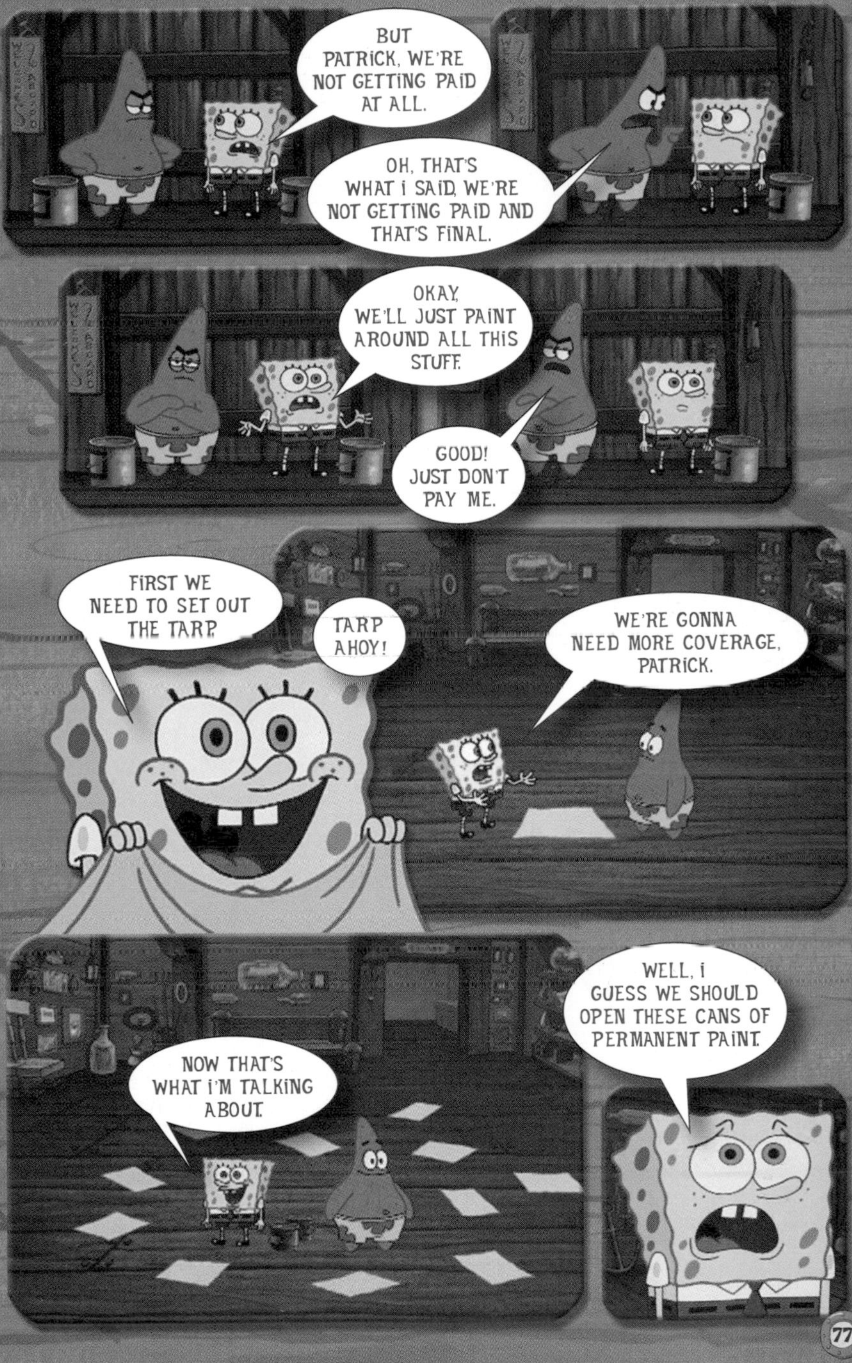

BUT PATRICK, WE'RE NOT GETTING PAID AT ALL.
OH, THAT'S WHAT I SAID, WE'RE NOT GETTING PAID AND THAT'S FINAL.
OKAY, WE'LL JUST PAINT AROUND ALL THIS STUFF.
GOOD! JUST DON'T PAY ME.
FIRST WE NEED TO SET OUT THE TARP.
TARP AHOY!
WE'RE GONNA NEED MORE COVERAGE, PATRICK.
NOW THAT'S WHAT I'M TALKING ABOUT.
WELL, I GUESS WE SHOULD OPEN THESE CANS OF PERMANENT PAINT.

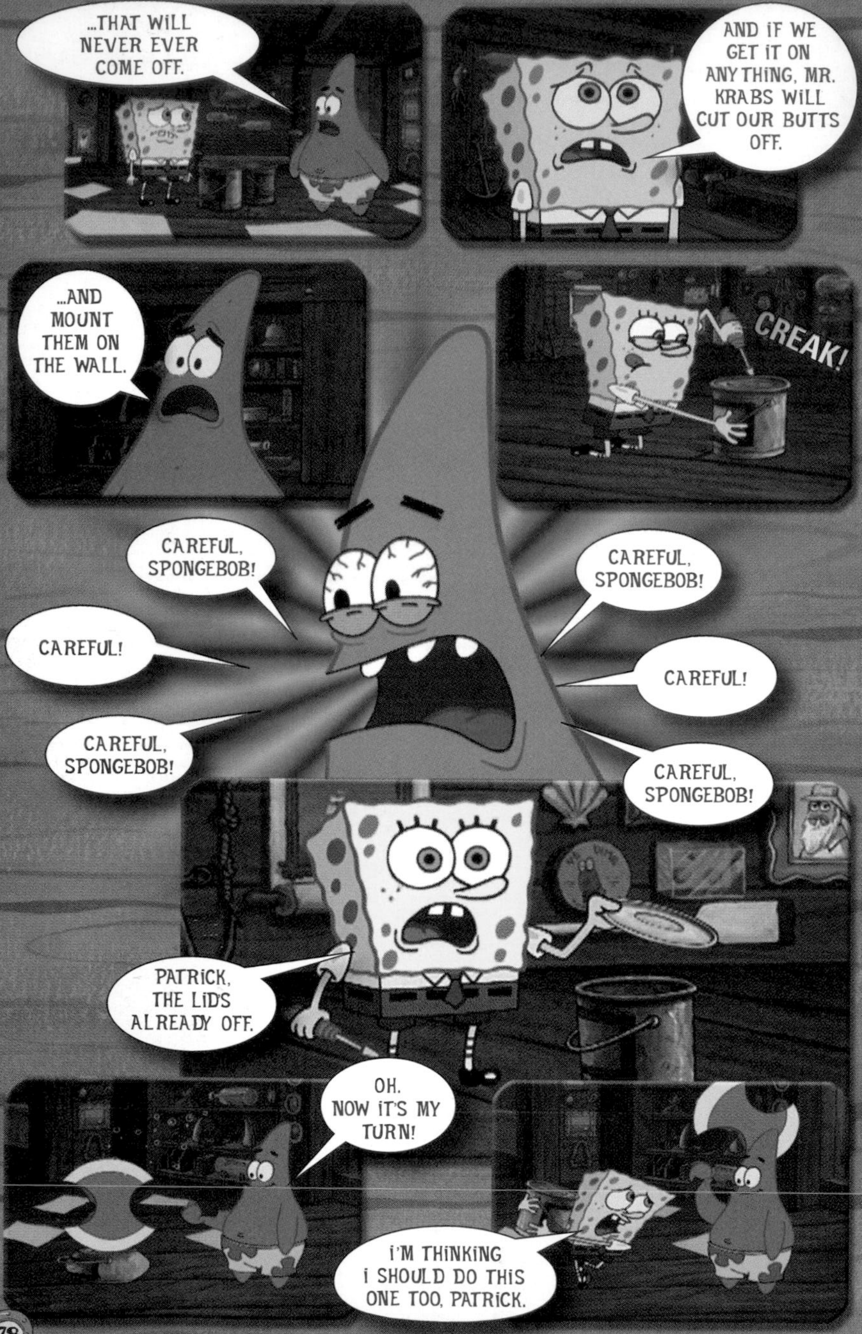
...THAT WILL NEVER EVER COME OFF.
AND IF WE GET IT ON ANYTHING, MR. KRABS WILL CUT OUR BUTTS OFF.
...AND MOUNT THEM ON THE WALL.
CREAK!
CAREFUL, SPONGEBOB!
CAREFUL, SPONGEBOB!
CAREFUL!
CAREFUL!
CAREFUL, SPONGEBOB!
CAREFUL, SPONGEBOB!
PATRICK, THE LID'S ALREADY OFF.
OH. NOW IT'S MY TURN!
I'M THINKING I SHOULD DO THIS ONE TOO, PATRICK.

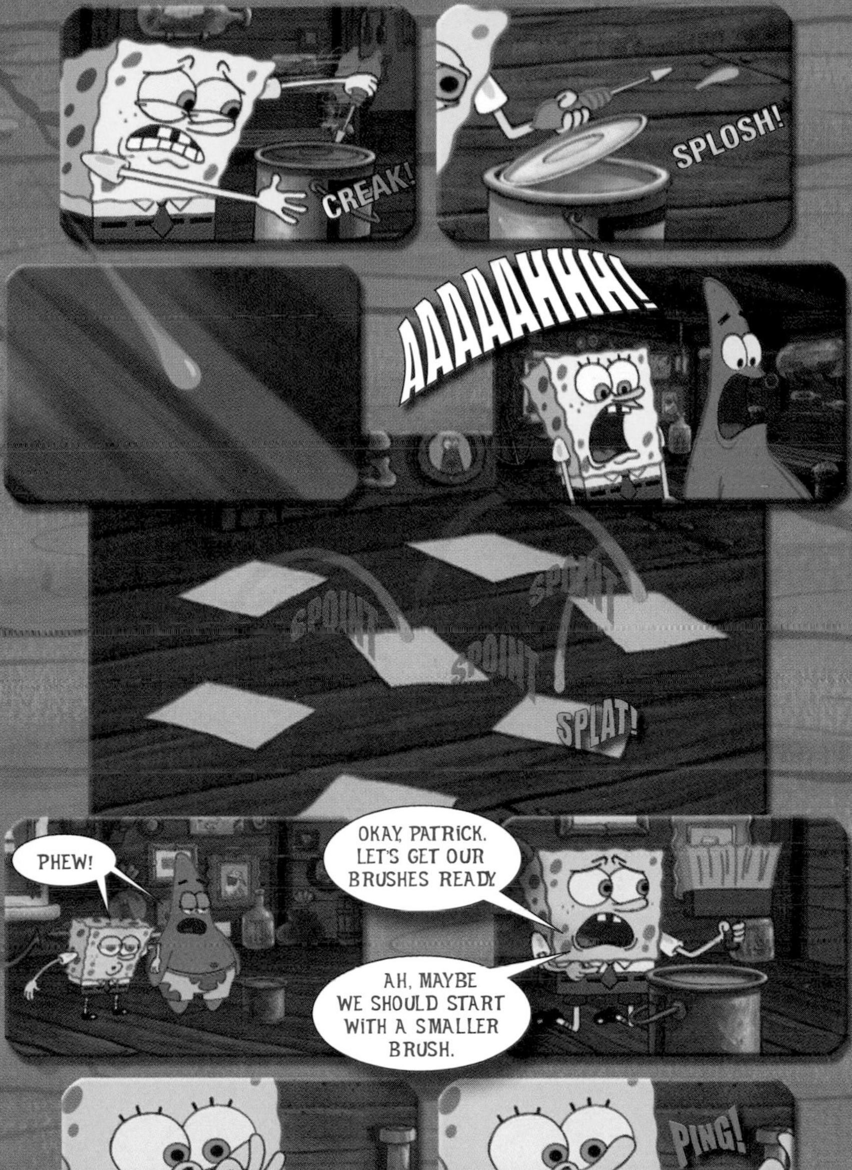
CREAK!
SPLOSH!
AAAAAHHH!
SPOINT
SPOINT
SPOINT
SPLAT!
PHEW!
OKAY, PATRICK. LET'S GET OUR BRUSHES READY.
AH, MAYBE WE SHOULD START WITH A SMALLER BRUSH.
PING!

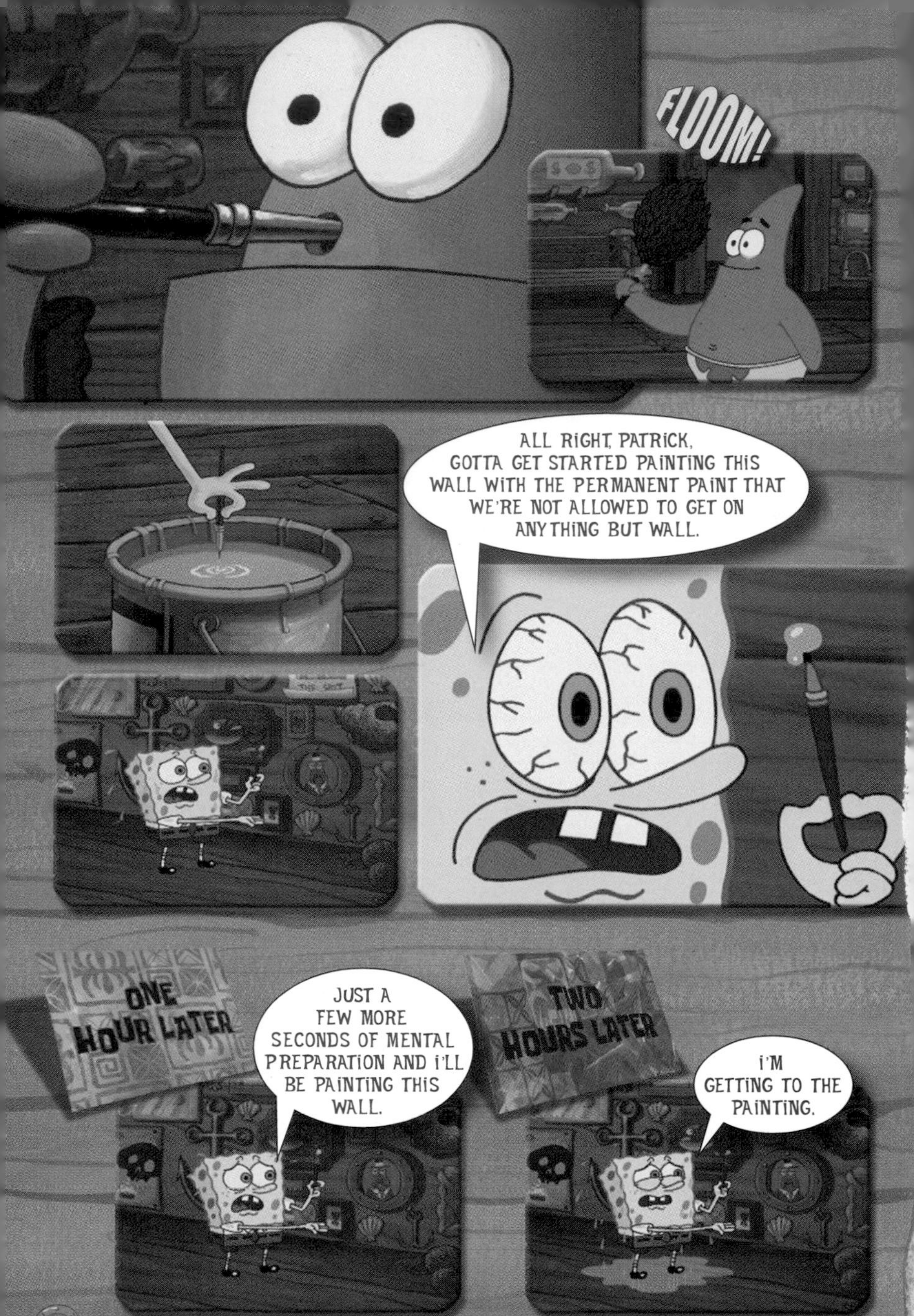
FLOOM!
ALL RIGHT, PATRICK, GOTTA GET STARTED PAINTING THIS WALL WITH THE PERMANENT PAINT THAT WE'RE NOT ALLOWED TO GET ON ANYTHING BUT WALL.
ONE HOUR LATER
JUST A FEW MORE SECONDS OF MENTAL PREPARATION AND I'LL BE PAINTING THIS WALL.
TWO HOURS LATER
I'M GETTING TO THE PAINTING.

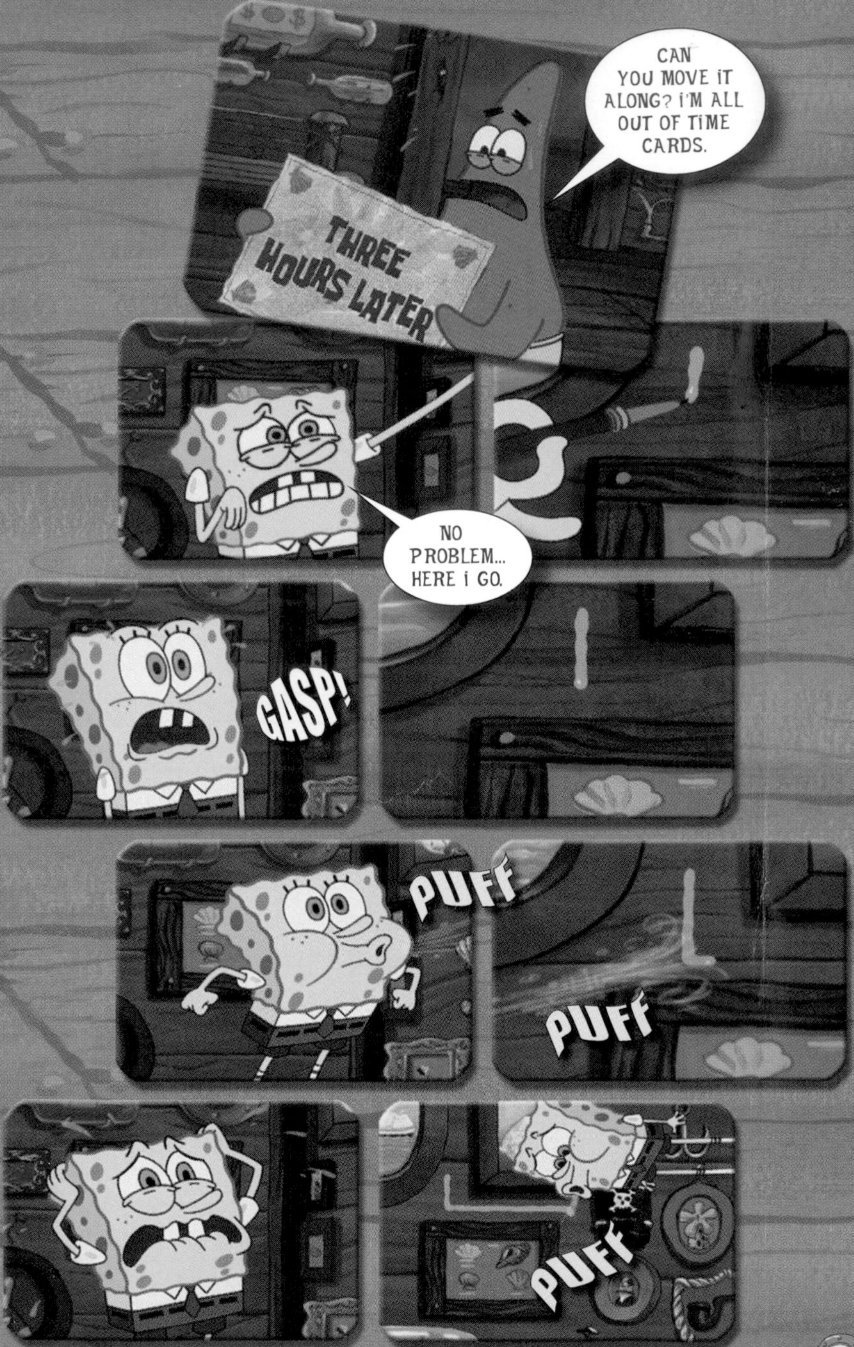
THREE HOURS LATER
CAN YOU MOVE IT ALONG? I'M ALL OUT OF TIME CARDS.
NO PROBLEM... HERE I GO.
GASP!
PUFF
PUFF
PUFF

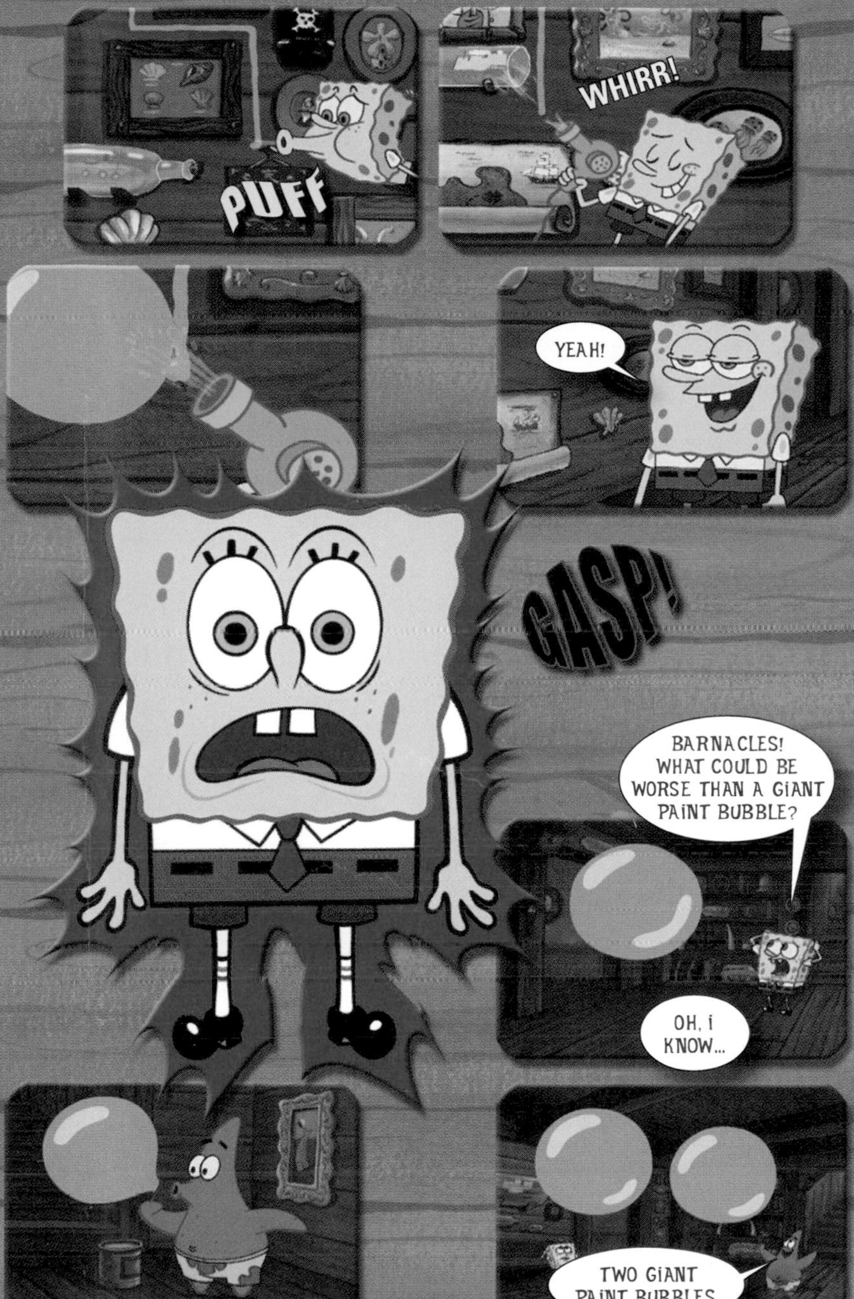
PUFF
WHIRR!
YEAH!
GASP!
BARNACLES! WHAT COULD BE WORSE THAN A GIANT PAINT BUBBLE?
OH, I KNOW...
TWO GIANT PAINT BUBBLES.

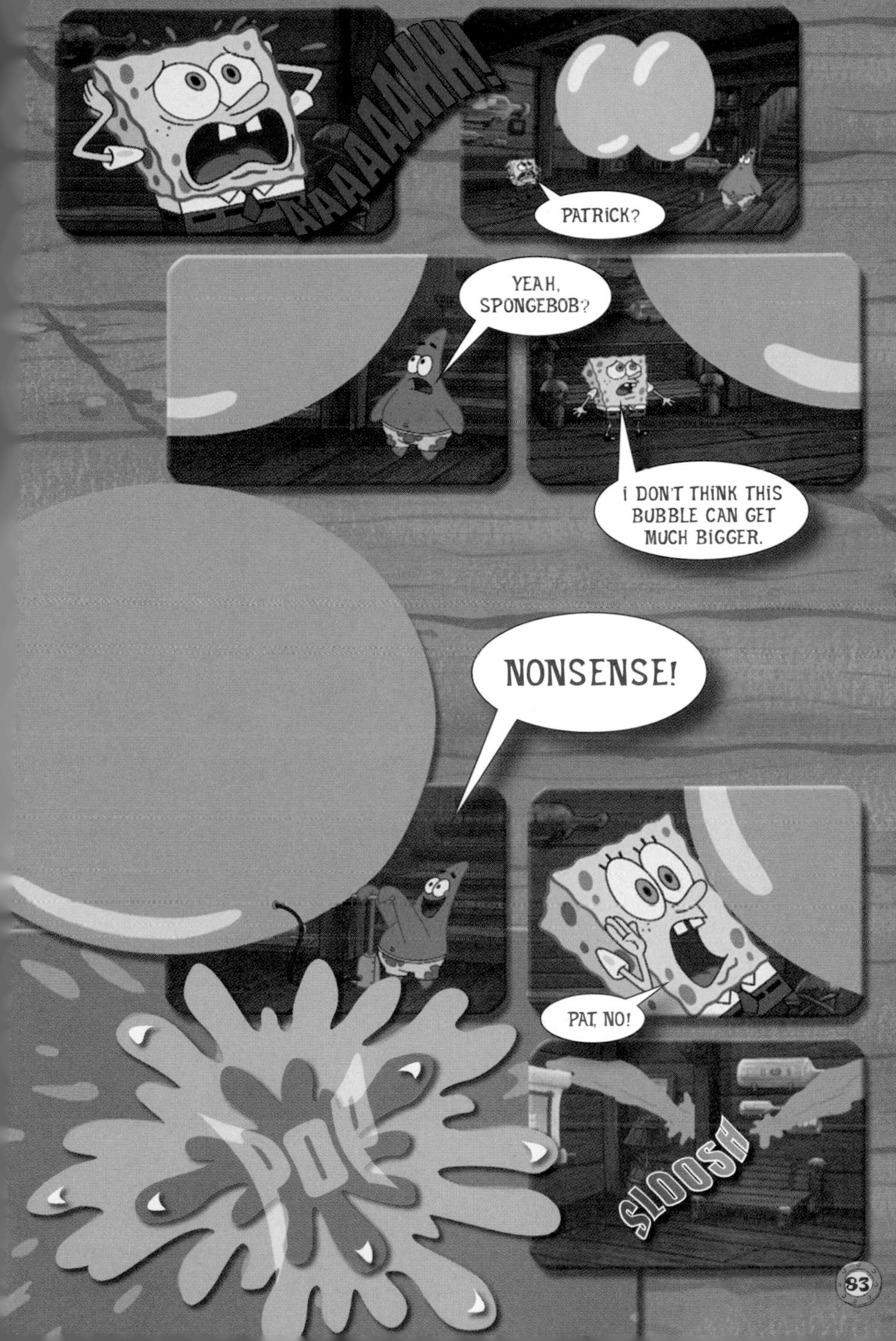
AAAAAAHHH!
PATRICK?
YEAH, SPONGEBOB?
I DON'T THINK THIS BUBBLE CAN GET MUCH BIGGER.
NONSENSE!
PAT, NO!
POP
SLOOSH

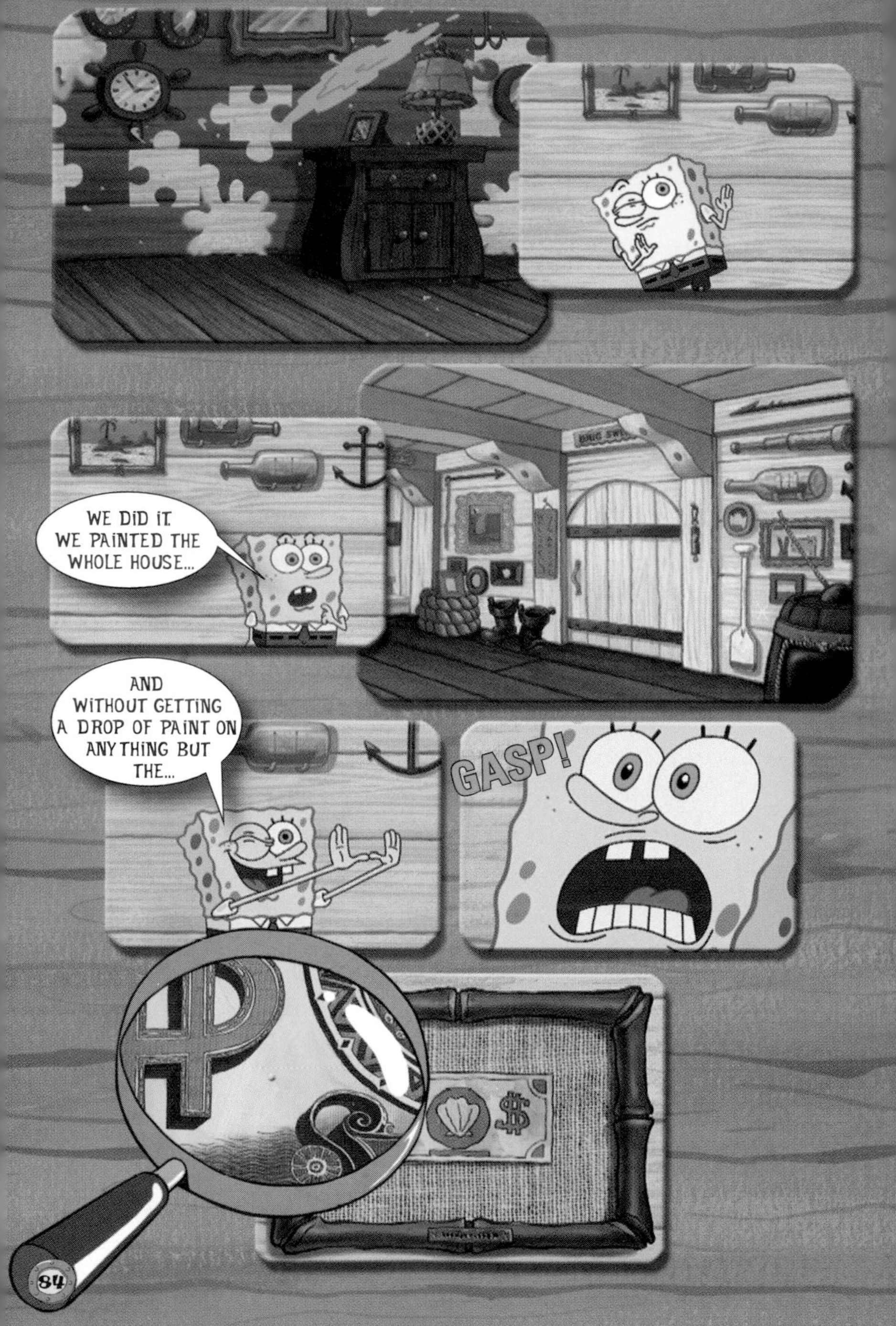
WE DID IT. WE PAINTED THE WHOLE HOUSE...
AND WITHOUT GETTING A DROP OF PAINT ON ANYTHING BUT THE...
GASP!

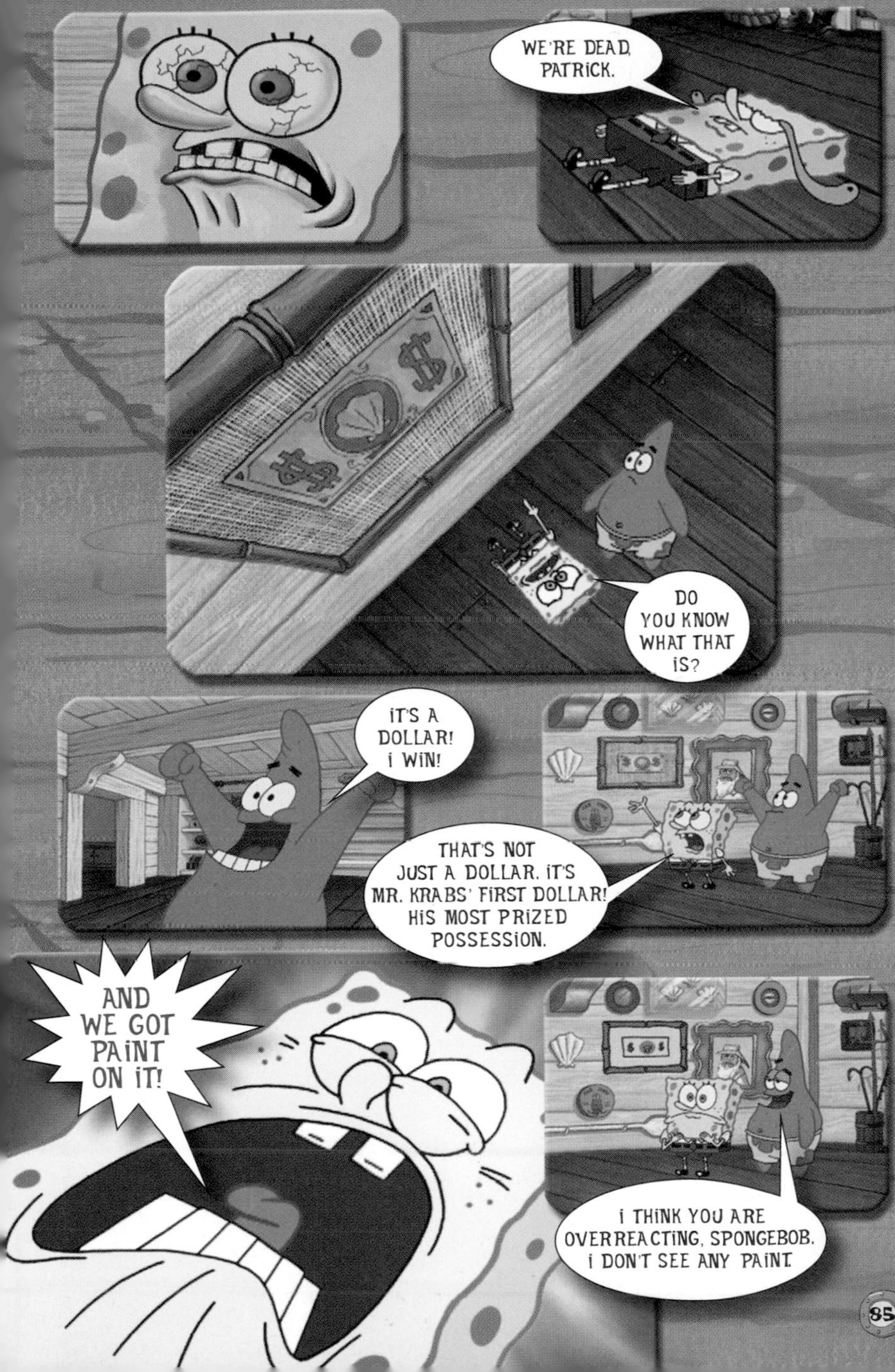

WE'RE DEAD, PATRICK.
DO YOU KNOW WHAT THAT IS?
IT'S A DOLLAR! I WIN!
THAT'S NOT JUST A DOLLAR. IT'S MR. KRABS' FIRST DOLLAR! HIS MOST PRIZED POSSESSION.
AND WE GOT PAINT ON IT!
I THINK YOU ARE OVERREACTING, SPONGEBOB. I DON'T SEE ANY PAINT.

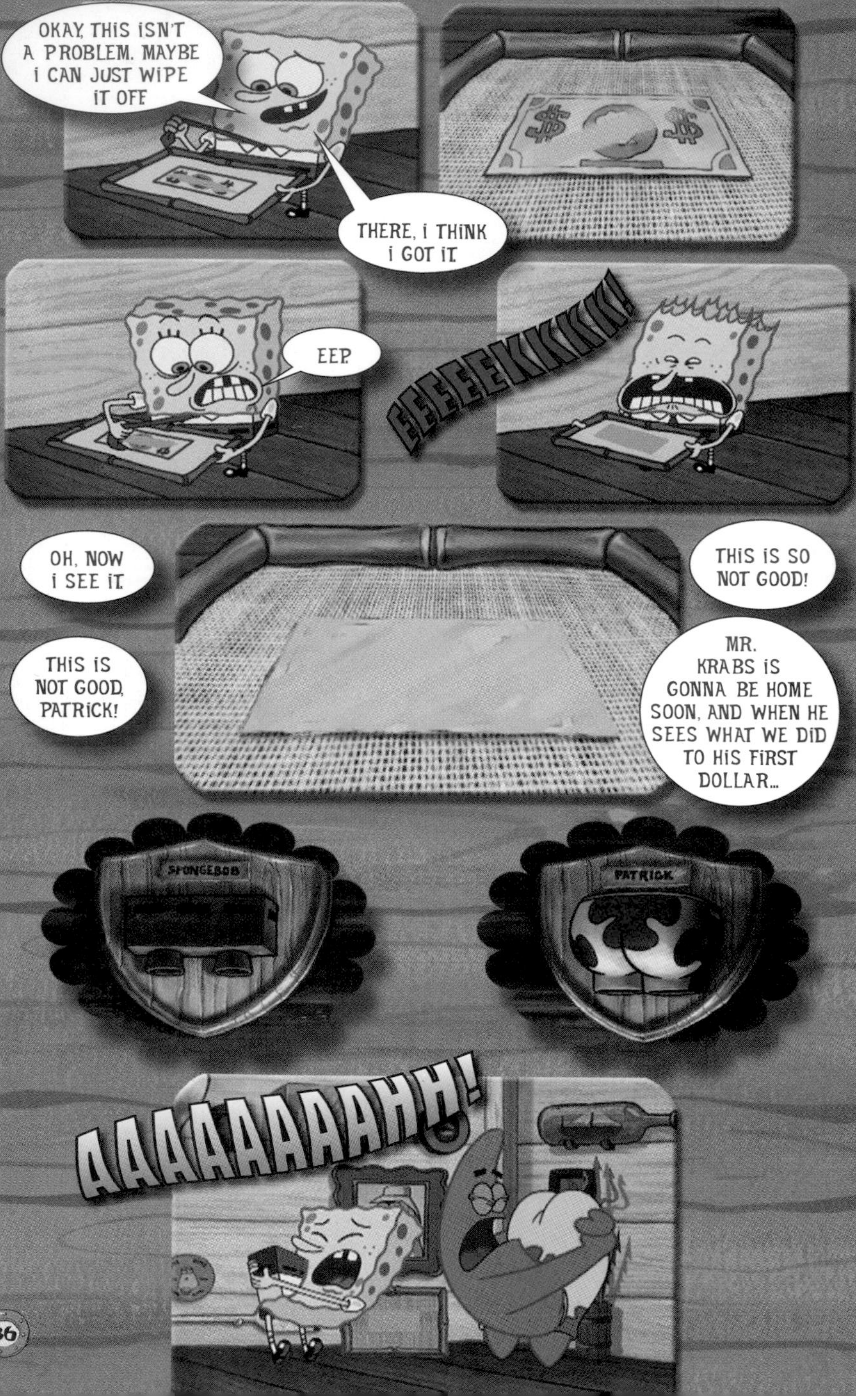
OKAY, THIS ISN'T A PROBLEM. MAYBE I CAN JUST WIPE IT OFF
THERE, I THINK I GOT IT.
EEP.
EEEEEKKKKKK!
OH, NOW I SEE IT.
THIS IS NOT GOOD, PATRICK!
THIS IS SO NOT GOOD!
MR. KRABS IS GONNA BE HOME SOON, AND WHEN HE SEES WHAT WE DID TO HIS FIRST DOLLAR...
SPONGEBOB
PATRICK
AAAAAAAAAHH!

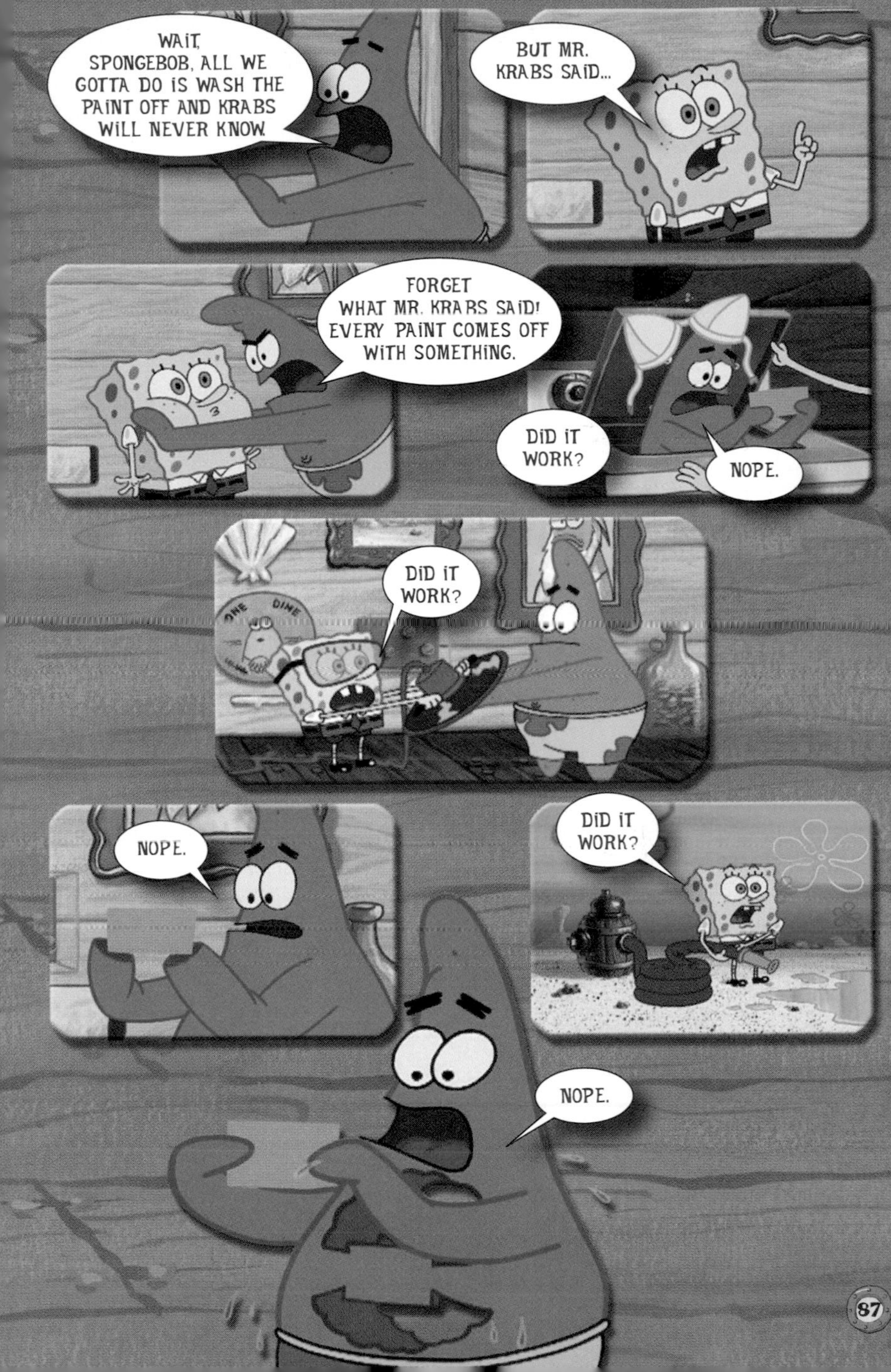
WAIT, SPONGEBOB, ALL WE GOTTA DO IS WASH THE PAINT OFF AND KRABS WILL NEVER KNOW.
BUT MR. KRABS SAID...
FORGET WHAT MR. KRABS SAID! EVERY PAINT COMES OFF WITH SOMETHING.
DID IT WORK?
NOPE.
DID IT WORK?
NOPE.
DID IT WORK?
NOPE.

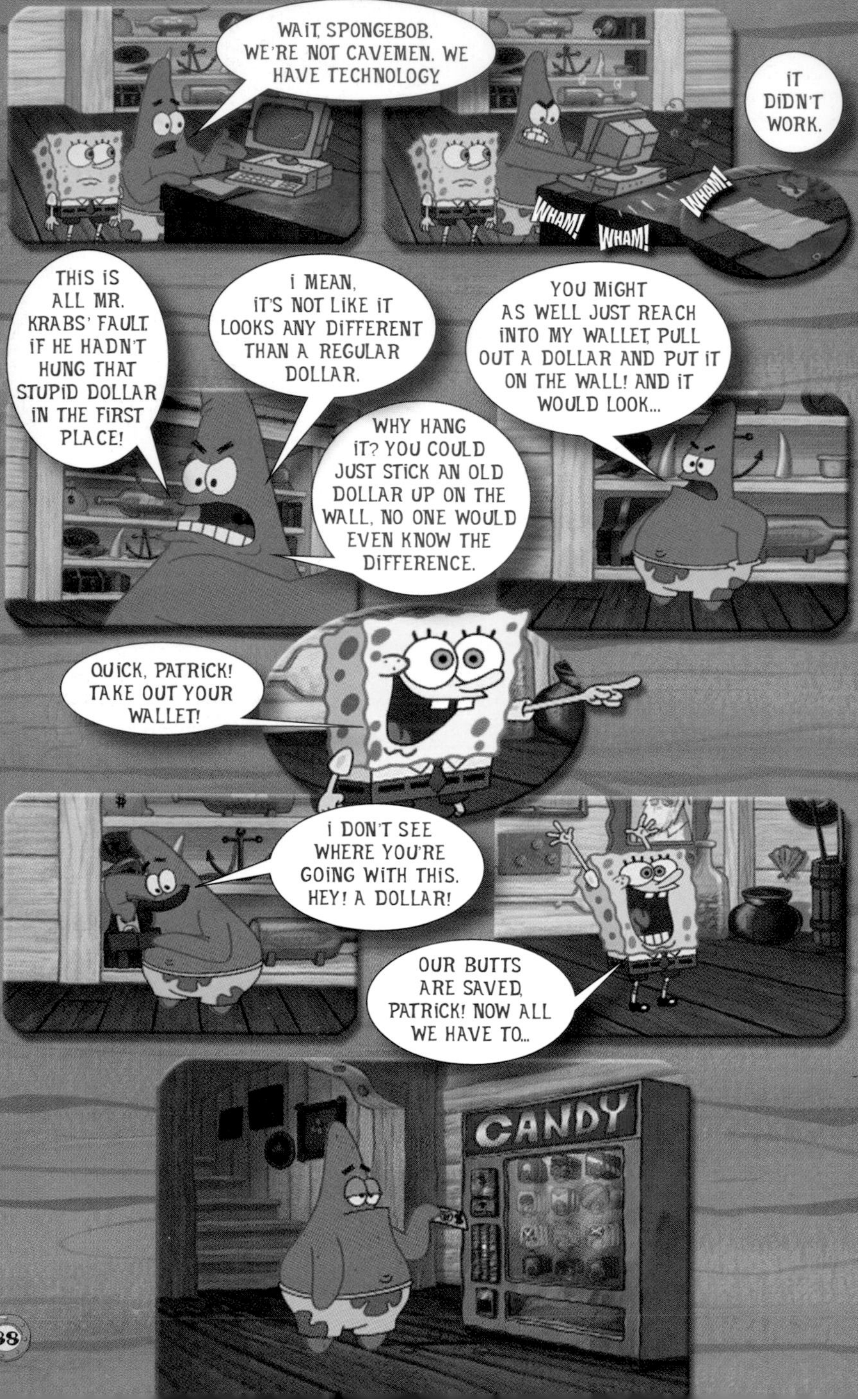
WAIT, SPONGEBOB. WE'RE NOT CAVEMEN. WE HAVE TECHNOLOGY.
IT DIDN'T WORK.
WHAM!
WHAM!
WHAM!
THIS IS ALL MR. KRABS' FAULT. IF HE HADN'T HUNG THAT STUPID DOLLAR IN THE FIRST PLACE!
I MEAN, IT'S NOT LIKE IT LOOKS ANY DIFFERENT THAN A REGULAR DOLLAR.
WHY HANG IT? YOU COULD JUST STICK AN OLD DOLLAR UP ON THE WALL, NO ONE WOULD EVEN KNOW THE DIFFERENCE.
YOU MIGHT AS WELL JUST REACH INTO MY WALLET, PULL OUT A DOLLAR AND PUT IT ON THE WALL! AND IT WOULD LOOK...
QUICK, PATRICK! TAKE OUT YOUR WALLET!
I DON'T SEE WHERE YOU'RE GOING WITH THIS. HEY! A DOLLAR!
OUR BUTTS ARE SAVED, PATRICK! NOW ALL WE HAVE TO...
CANDY

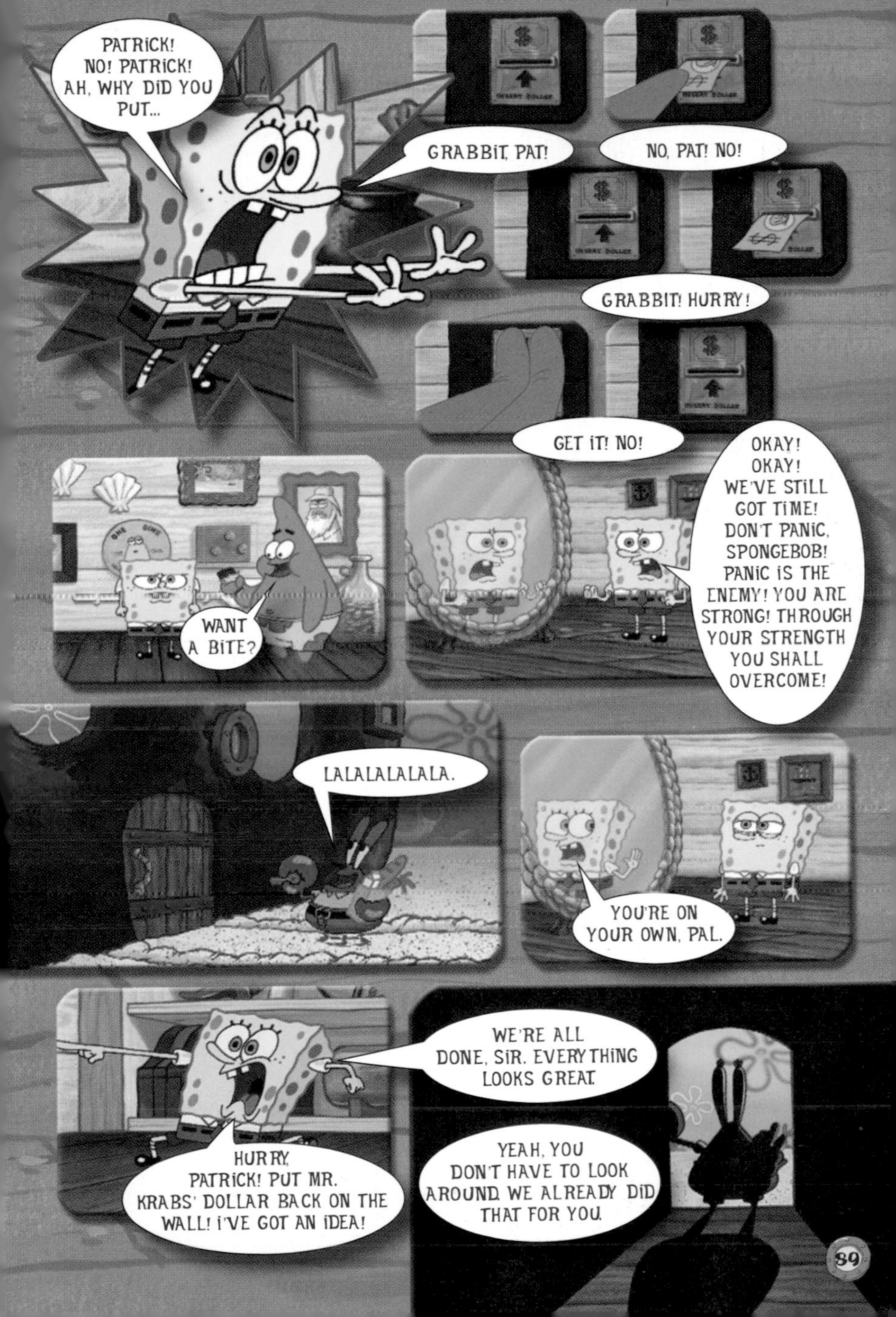
PATRICK! NO! PATRICK! AH, WHY DID YOU PUT...
GRABBIT, PAT!
NO, PAT! NO!
GRABBIT! HURRY!
GET IT! NO!
WANT A BITE?
OKAY! OKAY! WE'VE STILL GOT TIME! DON'T PANIC, SPONGEBOB! PANIC IS THE ENEMY! YOU ARE STRONG! THROUGH YOUR STRENGTH YOU SHALL OVERCOME!
LALALALALALA.
YOU'RE ON YOUR OWN, PAL.
WE'RE ALL DONE, SIR. EVERYTHING LOOKS GREAT.
HURRY, PATRICK! PUT MR. KRABS' DOLLAR BACK ON THE WALL! I'VE GOT AN IDEA!
YEAH, YOU DON'T HAVE TO LOOK AROUND. WE ALREADY DID THAT FOR YOU.

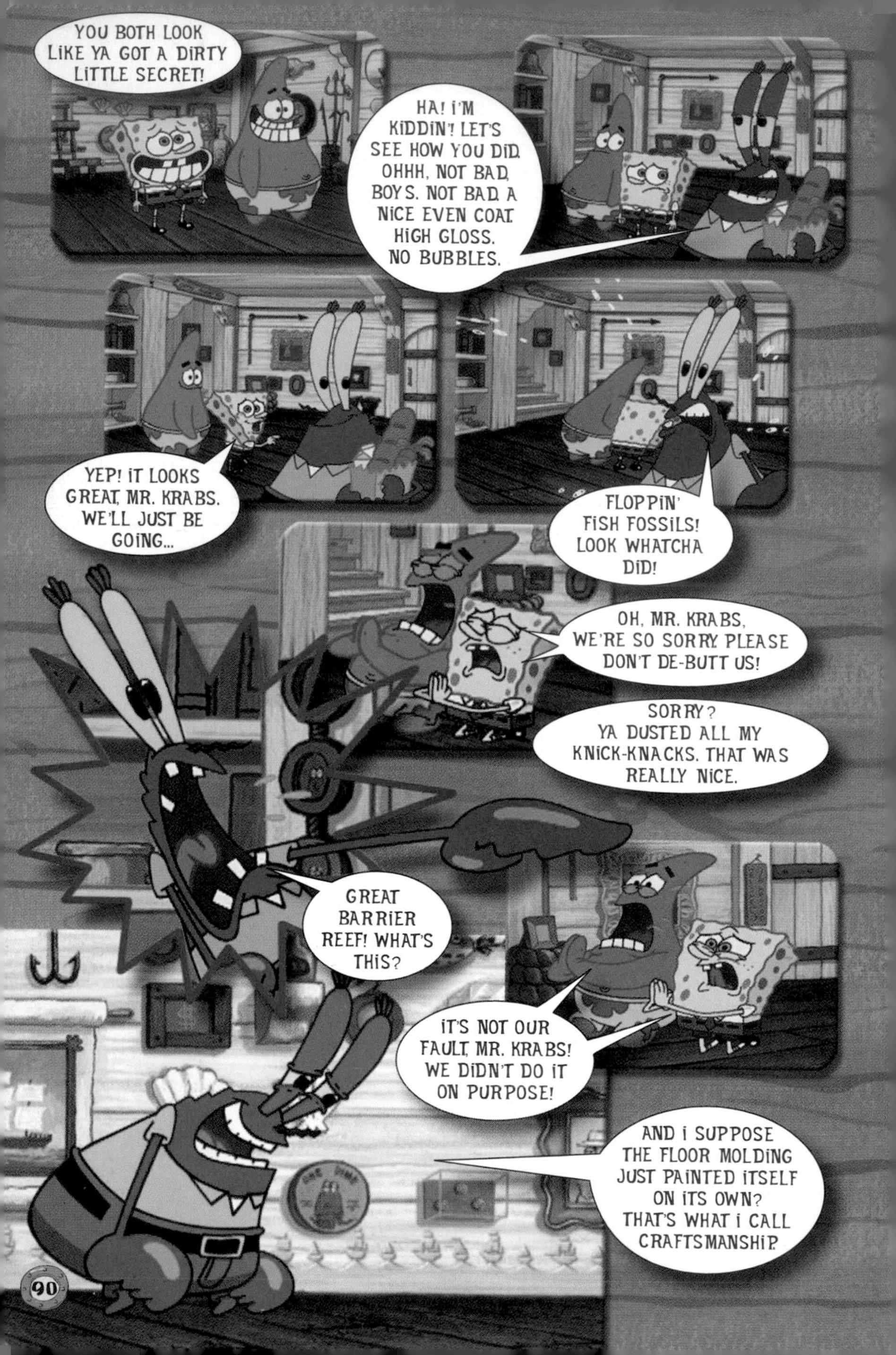
YOU BOTH LOOK LIKE YA GOT A DIRTY LITTLE SECRET!
HA! I'M KIDDIN'! LET'S SEE HOW YOU DID. OHHH, NOT BAD, BOYS. NOT BAD. A NICE EVEN COAT. HIGH GLOSS. NO BUBBLES.
YEP! IT LOOKS GREAT, MR. KRABS. WE'LL JUST BE GOING...
FLOPPIN' FISH FOSSILS! LOOK WHATCHA DID!
OH, MR. KRABS, WE'RE SO SORRY. PLEASE DON'T DE-BUTT US!
SORRY? YA DUSTED ALL MY KNICK-KNACKS. THAT WAS REALLY NICE.
GREAT BARRIER REEF! WHAT'S THIS?
IT'S NOT OUR FAULT, MR. KRABS! WE DIDN'T DO IT ON PURPOSE!
AND I SUPPOSE THE FLOOR MOLDING JUST PAINTED ITSELF ON ITS OWN? THAT'S WHAT I CALL CRAFTSMANSHIP.

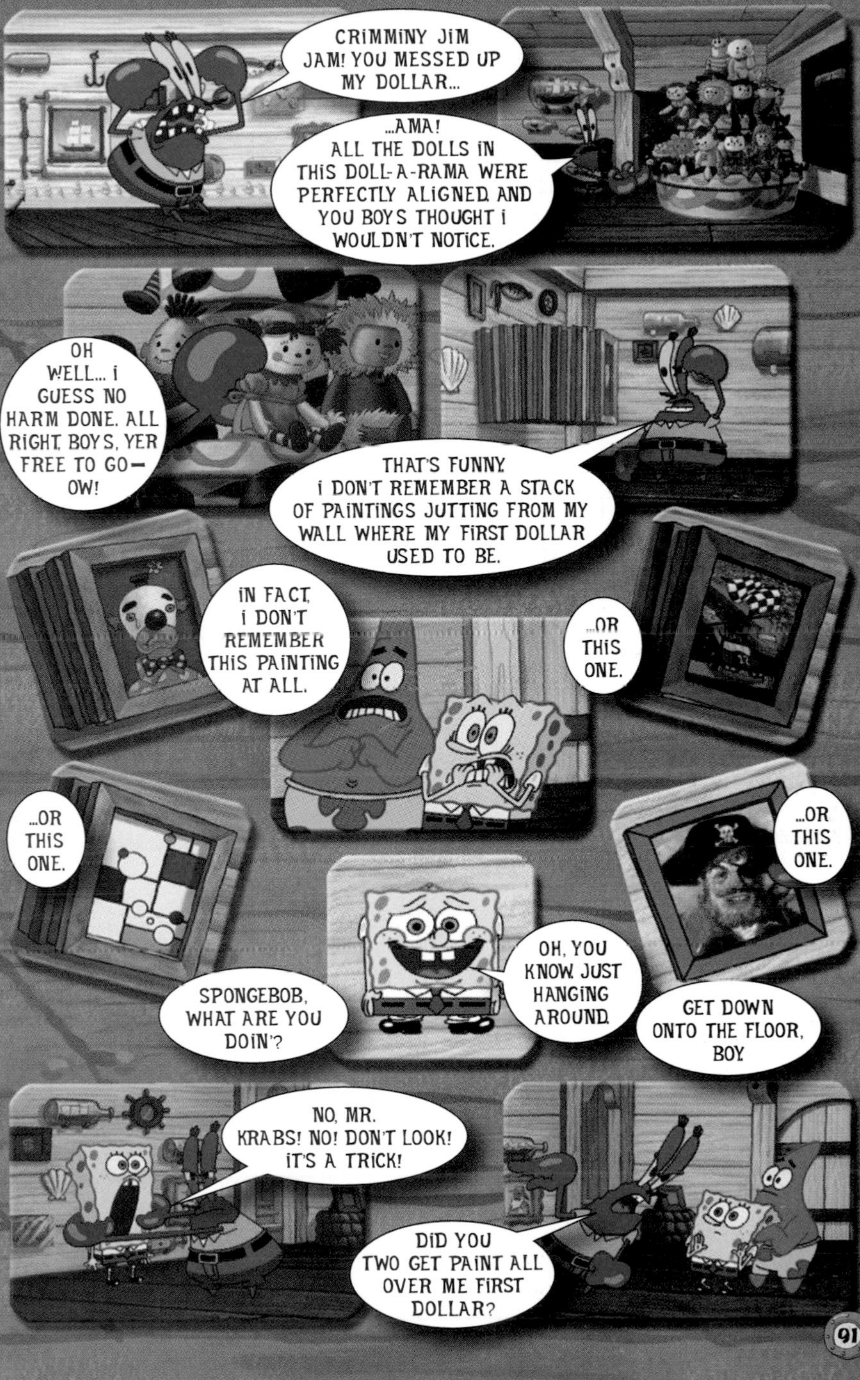
CRIMMINY JIM JAM! YOU MESSED UP MY DOLLAR...
...AMA! ALL THE DOLLS IN THIS DOLL-A-RAMA WERE PERFECTLY ALIGNED. AND YOU BOYS THOUGHT I WOULDN'T NOTICE.
OH WELL... I GUESS NO HARM DONE. ALL RIGHT, BOYS, YER FREE TO GO— OW!
THAT'S FUNNY. I DON'T REMEMBER A STACK OF PAINTINGS JUTTING FROM MY WALL WHERE MY FIRST DOLLAR USED TO BE.
IN FACT, I DON'T REMEMBER THIS PAINTING AT ALL.
...OR THIS ONE.
...OR THIS ONE.
...OR THIS ONE.
SPONGEBOB, WHAT ARE YOU DOIN'?
OH, YOU KNOW. JUST HANGING AROUND.
GET DOWN ONTO THE FLOOR, BOY.
NO, MR. KRABS! NO! DON'T LOOK! IT'S A TRICK!
DID YOU TWO GET PAINT ALL OVER ME FIRST DOLLAR?

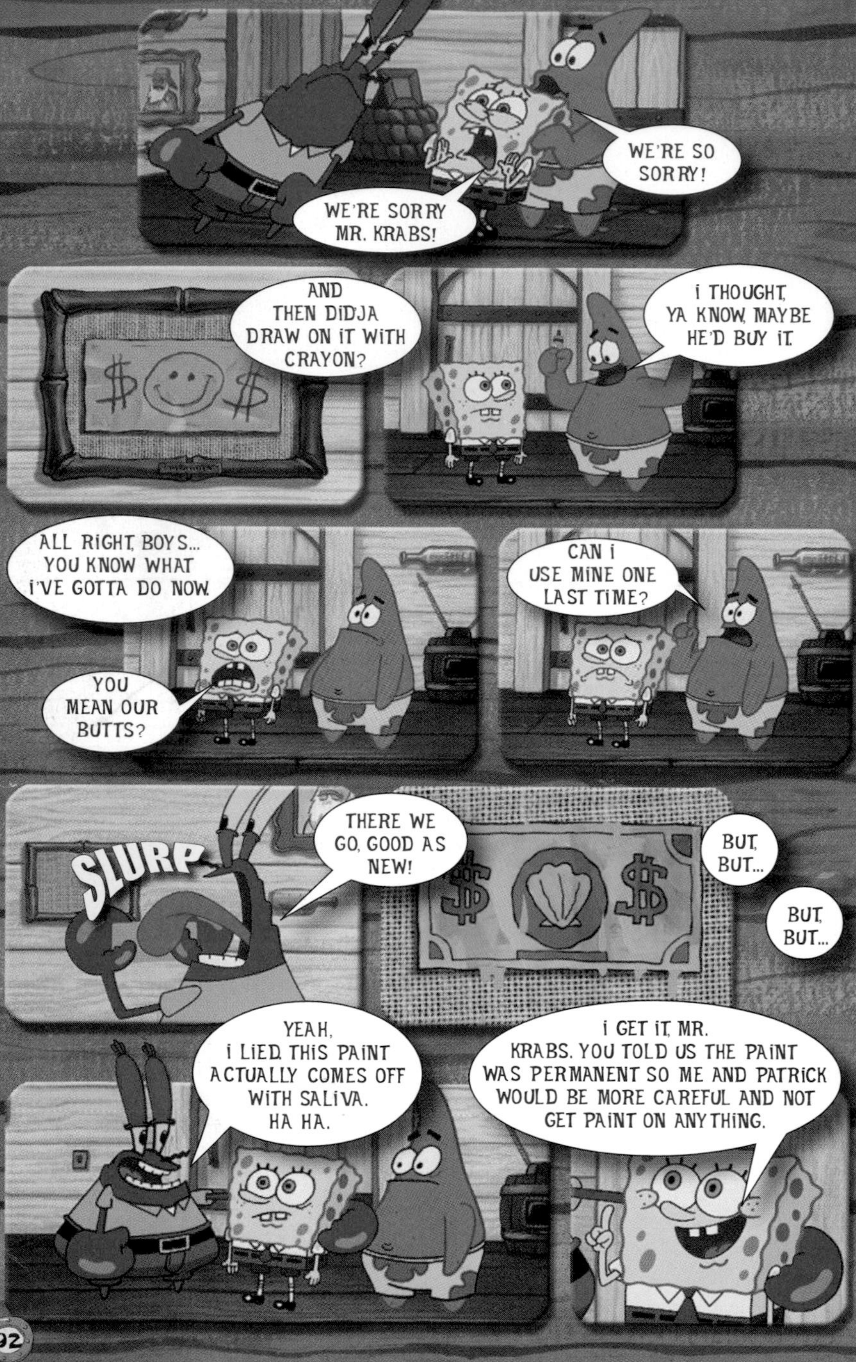
WE'RE SORRY MR. KRABS!
WE'RE SO SORRY!
AND THEN DIDJA DRAW ON IT WITH CRAYON?
I THOUGHT, YA KNOW, MAYBE HE'D BUY IT.
ALL RIGHT, BOYS... YOU KNOW WHAT I'VE GOTTA DO NOW.
YOU MEAN OUR BUTTS?
CAN I USE MINE ONE LAST TIME?
SLURP
THERE WE GO, GOOD AS NEW!
BUT, BUT...
BUT, BUT...
YEAH, I LIED. THIS PAINT ACTUALLY COMES OFF WITH SALIVA. HA HA.
I GET IT, MR. KRABS. YOU TOLD US THE PAINT WAS PERMANENT SO ME AND PATRICK WOULD BE MORE CAREFUL AND NOT GET PAINT ON ANYTHING.

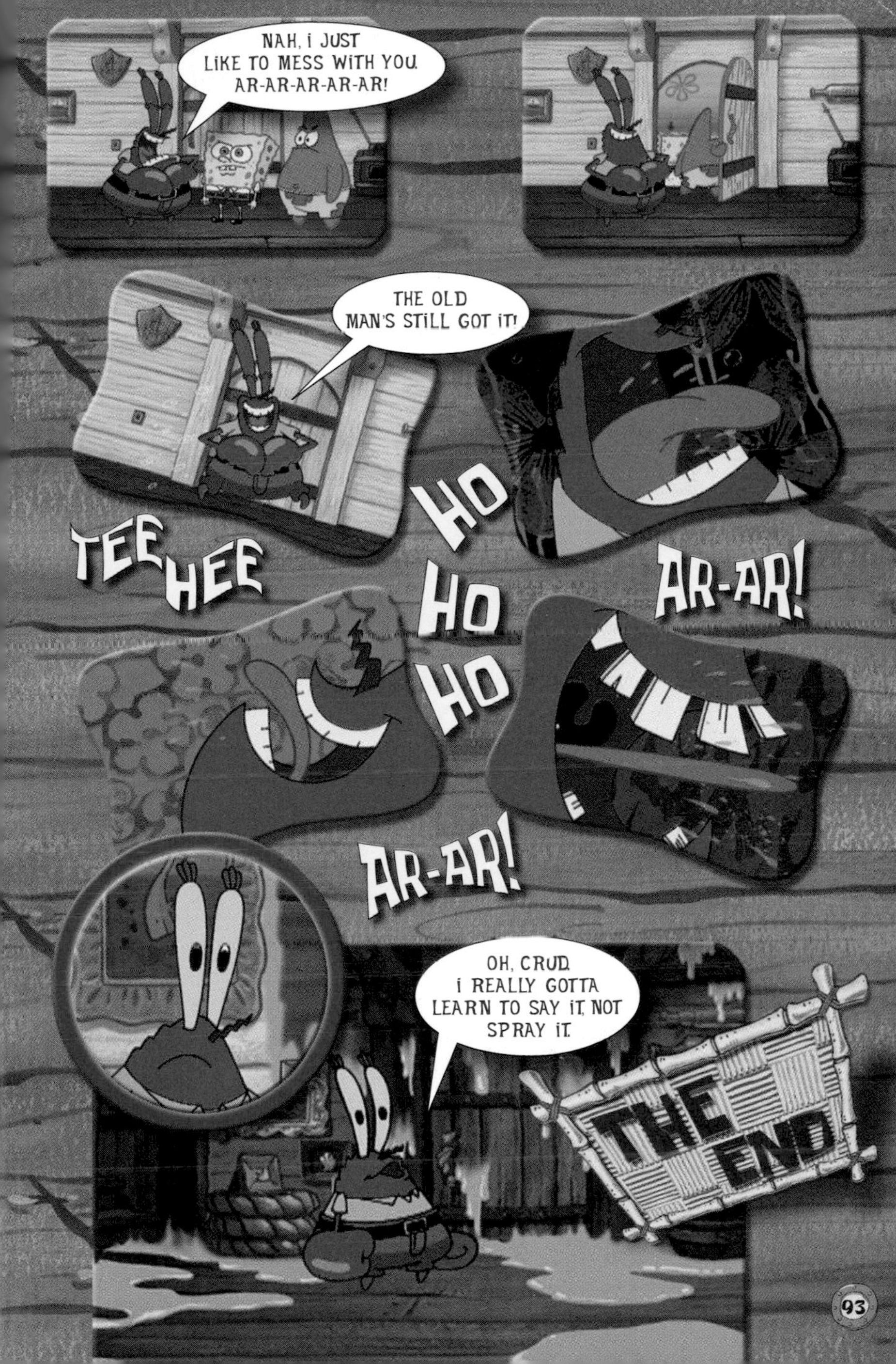

NAH, I JUST LIKE TO MESS WITH YOU. AR-AR-AR-AR-AR!
THE OLD MAN'S STILL GOT IT!
HO
TEE HEE
HO
AR-AR!
HO
AR-AR!
OH, CRUD. I REALLY GOTTA LEARN TO SAY IT, NOT SPRAY IT.
THE END

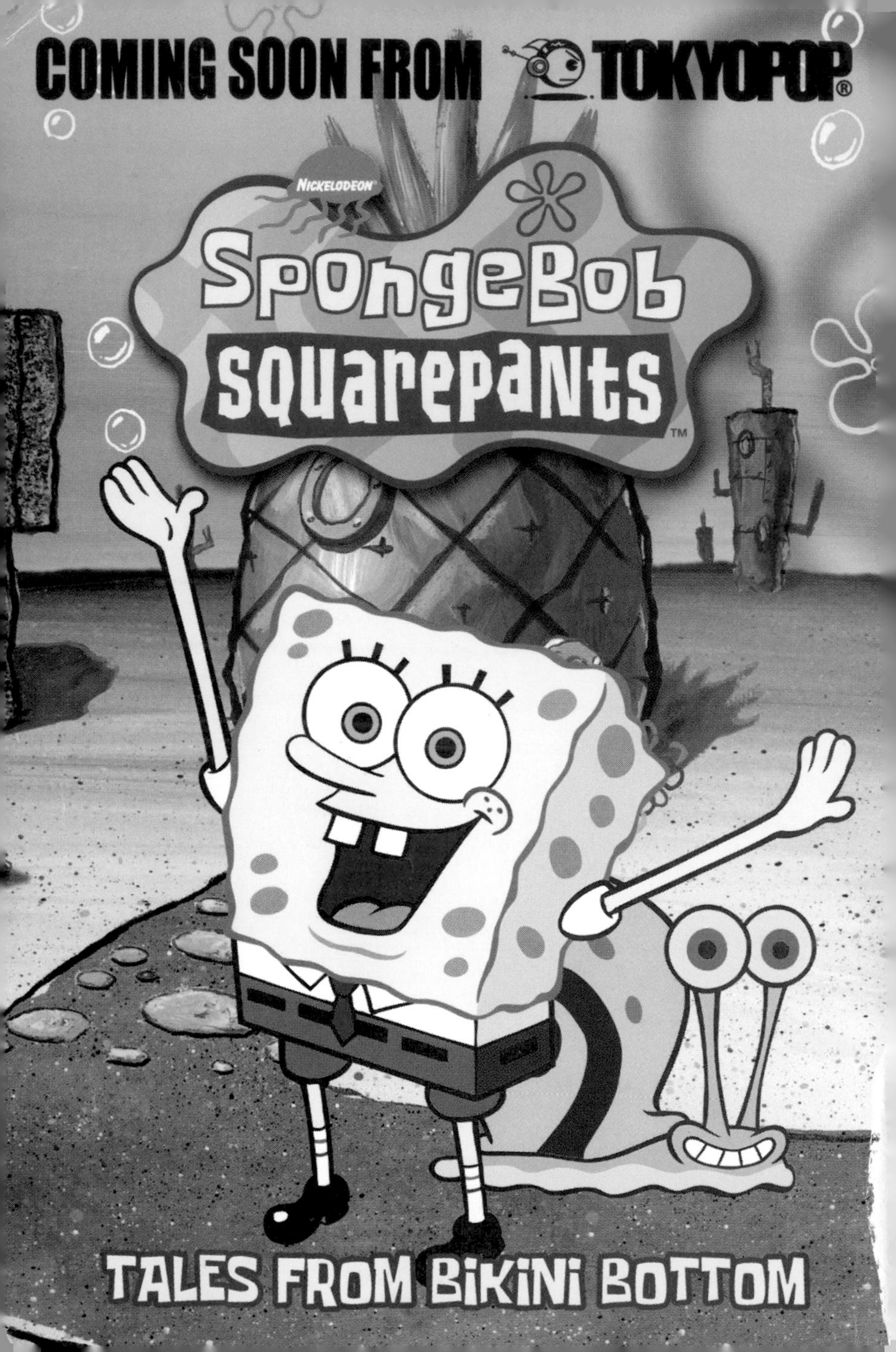
COMING SOON FROM
TOKYOPOP®
NICKELODEON
SpongeBob
SquarePants™
TALES FROM BIKINI BOTTOM

ALSO AVAILABLE FROM

MANGA

.HACK//LEGEND OF THE TWILIGHT
ANGELIC LAYER*
BABY BIRTH*
BRAIN POWERED*
BRIGADOON*
CARDCAPTOR SAKURA
CARDCAPTOR SAKURA: MASTER OF THE CLOW*
CHRONICLES OF THE CURSED SWORD
CLAMP SCHOOL DETECTIVES*
CLOVER
CORRECTOR YUI
COWBOY BEBOP*
COWBOY BEBOP: SHOOTING STAR*
CYBORG 009*
DEMON DIARY
DIGIMON*
DRAGON HUNTER
DRAGON KNIGHTS*
DUKLYON: CLAMP SCHOOL DEFENDERS*
FLCL*
FORBIDDEN DANCE*
GATE KEEPERS*
G GUNDAM*
GUNDAM WING
GUNDAM WING: BATTLEFIELD OF PACIFISTS
GUNDAM WING: ENDLESS WALTZ*
GUNDAM WING: THE LAST OUTPOST*
HARLEM BEAT
I.N.V.U.
INITIAL D*
JING: KING OF BANDITS*
JULINE
KARE KANO*
KINDAICHI CASE FILES, THE*
KODOCHA: SANA'S STAGE*
MAGIC KNIGHT RAYEARTH*
MAGIC KNIGHT RAYEARTH II* (COMING SOON)
MAN OF MANY FACES*

MARMALADE BOY*
MARS*
MIRACLE GIRLS
MONSTERS, INC.
PEACH GIRL
PEACH GIRL: CHANGE OF HEART*
PLANET LADDER*
PLANETES*
RAGNAROK
RAVE MASTER*
REALITY CHECK!
REBIRTH
REBOUND*
RISING STARS OF MANGA
SAILOR MOON
SAINT TAIL
SAMURAI GIRL: REAL BOUT HIGH SCHOOL*
SHAOLIN SISTERS*
SHIRAHIME-SYO: SNOW GODDESS TALES* (DEC. 2003)
THE SKULL MAN*
TOKYO MEW MEW*
VAMPIRE GAME*
WISH*
ZODIAC P.I.*

*INDICATES 100% AUTHENTIC MANGA (RIGHT-TO-LEFT FORMAT)

CINE-MANGA™

CARDCAPTORS
G. I. JOE SPY TROOPS
JACKIE CHAN ADVENTURES
JIMMY NEUTRON
KIM POSSIBLE
LIZZIE MCGUIRE
POWER RANGERS: NINJA STORM
SPONGEBOB SQUAREPANTS
SPY KIDS 2
TRANSFORMERS ARMADA

NOVELS

KARMA CLUB (APRIL 2004)
SAILOR MOON

TOKYOPOP KIDS

STRAY SHEEP

ART BOOKS

CARDCAPTOR SAKURA*
MAGIC KNIGHT RAYEARTH*

ANIME GUIDES

COWBOY BEBOP ANIME GUIDES
GUNDAM TECHNICAL MANUALS
SAILOR MOON SCOUT GUIDES

091003

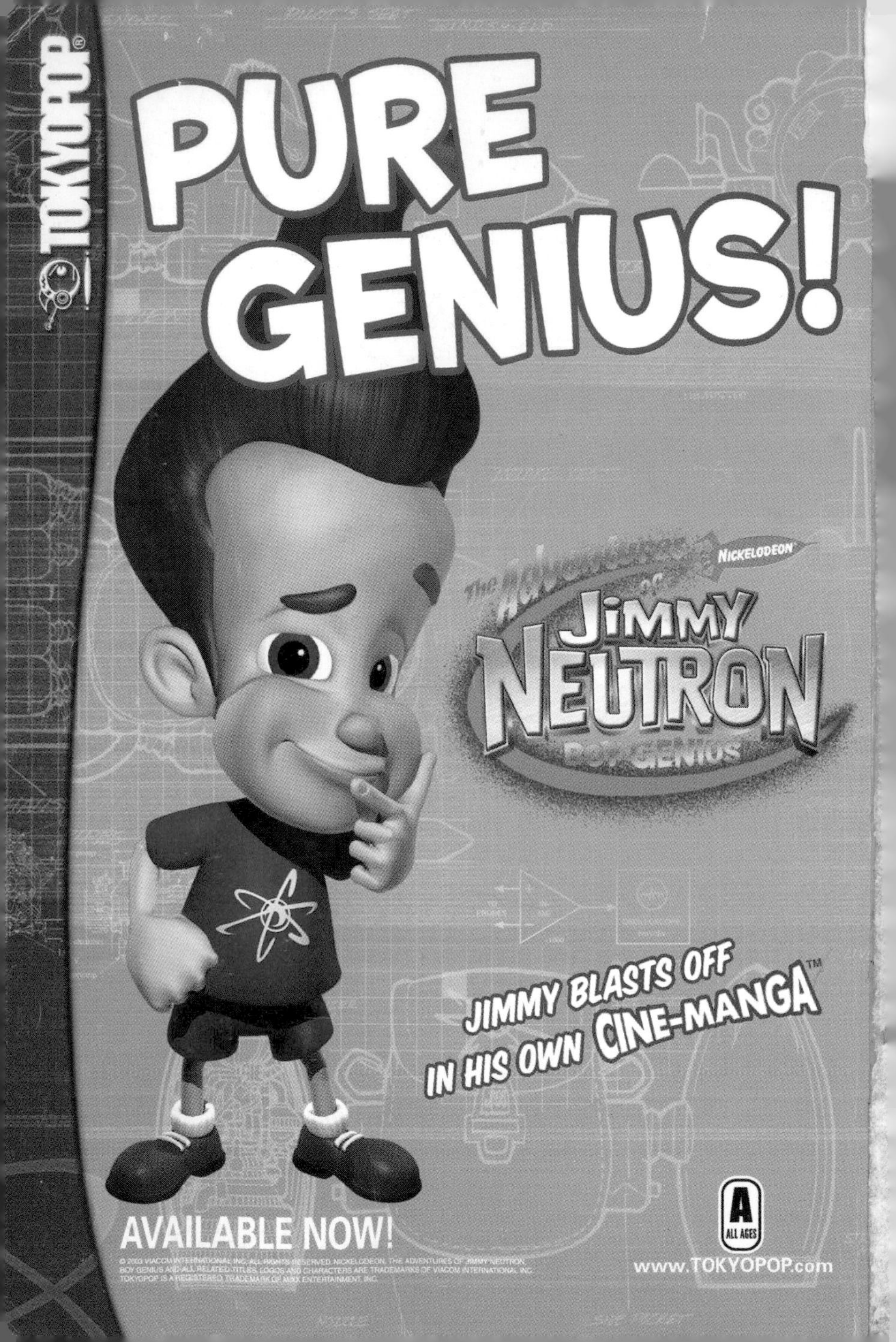